Junior
Worldmark
Encyclopedia of

World Holidays

Junior Worldmark Encyclopedia of

World Holidays

VOLUME 1

Buddha's Birthday,
Carnival,
Christmas

AN IMPRINT OF THE GALE GROUP

DETROIT · NEW YORK · SAN FRANCISCO
LONDON · BOSTON · WOODBRIDGE, CT

Junior Worldmark Encyclopedia of World Holidays

Robert H. Griffin and Ann H. Shurgin

Staff

Kelle Sisung, *Contributing Editor*
Carol DeKane Nagel, *U·X·L Managing Editor*
Thomas L. Romig, *U·X·L Publisher*
Meggin Condino, *Senior Analyst, New Product Development*

Dean Dauphinais, *Senior Editor, Imaging and Multimedia Content*
Shalice Shah-Caldwell, *Permissions Associate, Text and Pictures*

Robert Duncan, *Senior Imaging Specialist*
Randy A. Bassett, *Image Database Supervisor*
Barbara J. Yarrow, *Graphic Services Manager*

Pamela A. E. Galbreath, *Senior Art Director*
Graphix Group, *Typesetting*

Rita Wimberley, *Senior Buyer*
Evi Seoud, *Assistant Manager, Composition Purchasing and Electronic Prepress*
Dorothy Maki, *Manufacturing Manager*

Printed in the United States of America
10 9 8 7 6 5 4 3 2 1

Library of Congress Cataloging-in-Publication Data

Junior worldmark encyclopedia of world holidays/ edited by Robert Griffin.
    p. cm.
    Includes bibliographical references and index.
    Summary: Alphabetically arranged entries provide descriptions of celebrations around the world of some thirty holidays and festivals, including national and cultural holidays, such as Independence Day and New Year's Day, which are commemorated on different days for different reasons in a number of countries.
    ISBN 0-7876-3927-3 (set). — ISBN 0-7876-3928-1 (vol. 1). — ISBN 0-7876-3929-X (vol. 2). — ISBN 0-7876-3930-3 (vol. 3). — ISBN 0-7876-3931-1 (vol. 4).
    1. Holidays—Encyclopedias, Juvenile. 2. Festivals—Encyclopedias, Juvenile. [1. Holidays—Encyclopedias. 2. Festivals—Encyclopedias. 3. Encyclopedias and dictionaries.] I. Griffin, Robert H., 1951–

GT3933 .J86 2000
394.26'03—dc21

00-023425

Contents

Contents

Contents
by Country

Contents by Country

Reader's Guide

Ever wonder why children trick-or-treat on Halloween? How Christmas festivities in Italy differ from those in the United States? What the colors of Kwanzaa represent? When will Ramadan come this year? Who creates all those floats in the parades? The answers to these and other questions about holiday traditions and lore can be found in *Junior Worldmark Encyclopedia of World Holidays*. This four-volume set explores when, where, why, and how people from thirty countries around the world celebrate eleven different holidays.

Each chapter in *Junior Worldmark Encyclopedia of World Holidays* opens with a general overview of the featured holiday. The chapter then provides details on one to six countries that observe that holiday. Each overview and country profile is arranged into the following rubrics, allowing for quick scanning or comparisons among the countries and holidays:

- **Introduction:** Offers a brief description and useful background information on the holiday. The introduction in the overview discusses the holiday in general; the country introductions

focus on how the holiday is observed in that featured country.

- **History:** Discusses the holiday's development, often from ancient origins through modern times. When a holiday was established to commemorate a historical event, such as a revolution or a nation's declaration of independence, a historical account of the event is given. When a holiday began with the rise of a religion, a discussion of the growth of the religion follows. Each holiday's general history is presented in the overview, while its development in a particular country is the focus of the country history.

- **Folklore, Legends, Stories:** Each holiday has at least a few legends and stories, folklore and superstitions associated with it. These are discussed here, along with literature commonly associated with the holiday. Traditional characters or historical tales can be found, as well as a brief synopsis of a well-known story or an excerpt from a poem. Religious holidays include excerpts or synopses of the scriptural account on which they are based. For some holidays, sidebars listing popular stories and poems are included.

- **Customs, Traditions, Ceremonies:** This section delves into the actual celebration of the holiday, from preparation for its arrival through ceremonies to bid it farewell for another year. Some of the ceremonies and traditions are religious, others are secular. Some are based on beliefs and superstitions so old that no one knows their origin, while others center around the reenactment of historical or religious events. Some are carried out on a grand scale, while others involve a quiet family ceremony. Learn how a European family celebrates a particular holiday while someone in Africa or Asia celebrates it in a very different—or sometimes very similar—way.

- **Clothing, Costumes:** Some holidays, such as Halloween and Carnival, have costumes at the heart of the celebration. For others, such as Independence Days, simply wearing the national colors is enough. In many cultures, people don traditional folk costumes for particular holidays, while others just dress in their "Sunday best." Whether it is a pair of sneakers or a six-foot feather plume, clothing and costumes play an important role in the traditions. This section will explain how people dress for the holiday and why.

- **Foods, Recipes:** What does Christmas dinner mean to an Italian family? What do Chinese youngsters snack on at New Year festivals? What is the main "Thanksgiving dinner" dish in Swaziland? This rubric details the special holiday meals shared by people within a culture. It covers the foods themselves as well as table settings, mealtime ceremonies, and the significance of eating certain foods on special days. For some holidays, picnic or festival foods are also mentioned. For most countries, a favorite holiday recipe is featured.

- **Arts, Crafts, Games:** Described here are famous works of art associated with specific holidays, as well as crafts created by different peoples in connection with the holiday, such as intricate Nativity scenes made by Italian woodcarvers and special pictures created by Chinese artists to bring good luck in the New Year. Holiday decorations and traditional games are also discussed here. Included for some holidays are crafts projects that, in addition to bringing added enjoyment by making one's own decorations, will help foster an appreciation of the art of other cultures.

- **Symbols:** Included in the holiday overviews are discussions of the symbols associated with the holiday and its celebration. A description of each symbol is given, along with its origin, meaning, and significance to the holiday.

- **Music, Dance:** Whether performing classical compositions or folk dancing in a courtyard, people all over the world love to make music and dance during their holidays. This rubric focuses on the music and dance that helps make up holiday celebrations. Some musical performances can be fiercely competitive, like the steel band contests held during Carnival in Trinidad. Others are solemn and deeply moving, like a performance of Handel's *Messiah* in a cathedral at Easter. Here learn about folk instruments, the origins of songs and dances, and famous composers or musicians from many cultures. Excerpts from songs associated with the holiday are also given.

- **Special Role of Children, Young Adults:** Children and young adults often have a special role to play in holiday celebrations. While children may simply participate in family activities during a holiday in some countries, in others children have distinct roles in parades, plays and performances, or customs. Here students can learn how children their own age celebrate holidays in nations thousands of miles away.

- **For More Information and Sources:** Print and electronic sources for further study are found at the end of each holiday overview and again at the end of each country essay. Those following the overview are general sources for the holiday, whereas the others pertain to a particular nation. Books listed should be able to be found in a library, and electronic sources are accessible on the World Wide Web.

Additionally, each chapter contains a Holiday Fact Box highlighting the themes of the specific holiday, while sprinkled throughout the set are boxes featuring recipes, activities, and more fascinating facts. One hundred twenty-five photos help bring the festivities to life. Beginning each volume is a table of contents for the entire set listing the holidays and countries featured, a table of contents by country, an explanation of how the modern calendar

developed, a calendar list of world holidays, and a words to know section. Concluding each volume is a cumulative subject index providing easy access to the holidays, countries, traditions, and topics discussed throughout *Junior Worldmark Encyclopedia of World Holidays*.

Advisory Board

Special thanks to the *Junior Worldmark Encyclopedia of World Holidays* advisors for their invaluable comments and suggestions:

- Mary Alice Anderson, Media Specialist, Winona Middle School, Winona, Minnesota.

- Ginny Ayers, Department Chair, Media Technology Services, Evanston Township High School, Evanston, Illinois.

- Jonathan Betz-Zall, Children's Librarian, Sno-Isle Regional Library System, Edmonds, Washington.

- Peter Butts, Media Specialist, East Middle School, Holland, Michigan.

Comments and Suggestions

We welcome your comments on this work as well as your suggestions for holidays to be featured in future editions of *Junior Worldmark Encyclopedia of World Holidays*. Please write: Editors, *Junior Worldmark Encyclopedia of World Holidays*, U•X•L, 27500 Drake Rd., Farmington Hills, MI 48331–3535; call toll-free: 1–800–877–4253; fax: 248–414–5043; or send e-mail via www. galegroup.com.

How the Modern Calendar Developed

The Egyptian Calendar

The earliest known calendar, that of the Egyptians, was lunar based, or calculated by the cycles of the Moon. One cycle is a lunar month, about 29.5 days in length, the time it takes the Moon to revolve once around the Earth. Although the calculations are fairly simple, reliance upon lunar months eventually leads to a problem: a lunar year, based upon 12 lunar cycles, is only 354 days. This is 11 days shorter than the solar year, the time it takes Earth to revolve once around the Sun. In any agricultural society, such as that of ancient Egypt, the solar-based seasons of the year are vitally important: they are the most reliable guide for knowing when to plow, plant, harvest, or store agricultural produce. Obviously, the discrepancy between the lunar and solar year had to be addressed.

The Egyptian solution was to rely on a solar calendar to govern civil affairs and agriculture; this was put in place around the third millennium B.C. This calendar observed the same new year's day as the older lunar one, which for the Egyptians was the day, about July 3, of the appearance on the horizon just before sunrise of the star Sirius, the "Dog Star." This event was significant for the Egyptians, for it occurred at nearly the same time the Nile River flooded each year, the key to their agricultural prosperity. The new Egyptian solar calendar also retained the division of days into months, although they were no longer based on lunar cycles. The Egyptian year in the reformed calendar contained 12 months of 30 days, with 5 days added throughout the year, bringing the total number of days to 365. It was only a fraction of a day different from the length of the solar year as determined by modern scientific means.

The Sumerian Calendar

Like the early Egyptian calendar, the ancient Sumerian calendar, developed around the twenty–seventh century B.C., was lunar. To the Sumerians, however, the Moon's cycles were apparently more significant, for they retained lunar months and a 354–day year. They made alignments with the seasons by adding extra days outside the regular calendar. (This process of adding extra days as necessary to reconcile the lunar with the solar year is called intercalation.) The calendar of the sacred city of Nippur, which became the Sumerian standard in the eighteenth century B.C., assigned names to the months, with the intercalary month designated by royal decree.

The Seven–day Week

The ancient Babylonians, a Sumerian people with a highly developed astronomy, are thought to be the first people to observe a seven-day week. The concept was probably based upon the periods between the distinct phases of the moon, which roughly correspond to seven days. The Babylonians also regarded the number seven as sacred, probably because they knew of seven principal heavenly bodies—Sun, Moon, Mars, Mercury, Jupiter, Venus, and Saturn—and saw supernatural significance in their seemingly wild movements against a backdrop of fixed stars. The days of the week were named for these principal heavenly bodies, one assigned to each day according to which governed the first hour of that day.

In addition to their lunar calendar, the Babylonians also devised a solar calendar based upon the points at which the Sun rises in relation to the constellations. This calendar is the basis for the zodiac system, the key to astrology.

From the Babylonians, the ancient Hebrews are believed to have adopted the practices of intercalation and observance of a seven-day week, probably during the time of Jewish captivity in Babylon beginning in 586 B.C. Babylonian influence may also have played a role in their observing every seventh day as special—the Jewish concept of Sabbath. Evidence for an earlier Jewish calendar (from at least the twelfth century B.C.)

does exist, however; thus, the observance of a Sabbath may well have existed before the Babylonian captivity. In any event, it is clear that the tradition of the seven-day week, as well as the retention of the concept of months, has much to do with the Western inheritance of Jewish calendar practices. (See also **The Hebrew Calendar**, below.)

The seven-day week as we know it today was carried into Christian use in the first century A.D. and was officially adopted by the Roman emperor Constantine in the fourth century. Interestingly, the English names for the days still reflect their origin in the names of the seven principal heavenly bodies of the ancient Babylonian astronomy:

- **Sunday:** Old English *Sunnan daeg*, a translation of Latin *dies solis*, "day of the sun."

- **Monday:** Old English *Monan daeg*, a translation of Latin *lunae dies*, "day of the moon"; compare with the French *lundi*.

- **Tuesday:** Old English *Tiwes daeg*, "day of Tiw," an adaptation of Latin *dies Martis*, "day of Mars" (the god Tiw being identified with the Roman Mars); compare with the French *Mardi*.

- **Wednesday:** Old English *Wodnes daeg*, "Woden's Day," an adaptation of Latin *Mercurii dies*, "day of Mercury" (the god Woden being identified with the Roman Mercury); compare with the French *mercredi*.

- **Thursday:** Old English *Thunres daeg*, "Thunor's day" or "Thor's day," an adaptation of the Latin *dies Jovis*, "day of Jove" (the god Thor being identified with the Roman Jove); compare with the French *jeudi*.

- **Friday:** Old English *Frize daeg*, "Freya's Day," an adaptation of the Latin *dies Veneris*, "day of Venus" (the goddess Freya being identified with the Roman Venus); compare with the French *vendredi*.

- **Saturday:** Old English *Saetern(es) daeg*, derived from the Latin *Saturni Dies*, "day of Saturn."

The Hebrew Calendar

Little is known of the Hebrew calendar prior to the Exodus from Egypt (c. 1250 B.C.) except that it appears to have contained four single and four double months called *yereah*. The early Hebrews apparently did not study the heavens and timekeeping as did their Sumerian and Egyptian neighbors. In fact, it was only after the period of Babylonian exile (586–516 B.C.) that a more fully developed method of timekeeping was adopted to modify the ancient practices. After their return from captivity, the Hebrews employed a calendar very similar to that of the Babylonians, intercalating (adding as necessary) months into the lunar calendar so it would correspond with the solar year. Unlike the Babylonians, who marked the beginning of the new year in the spring, the Hebrews retained the custom of recognizing the new year in the autumn, the time of their principal religious festivals of Rosh Hashanah (New Year), Yom Kippur, the Sukkoth, all falling in the month of Tishri (September/October). Still, similarities between the Jewish and Babylonian calendars are clear from a comparison of the names used in each system for the months:

Names of the Months in the Babylonian and Jewish Calendar Systems

Babylonian	Jewish	Equivalent
Nisanu	Nisan	March/April
Aiaru	Iyar	April/May
Simanu	Sivan	May/June
Du'uzu	Tammuz	June/July
Abu	Ab	July/August
Ululu	Elul	August/September
Tashritu	Tishri	September/October
Arahsamnu	Heshvan	October/November
Kislimu	Kislev	November/December
Tebetu	Tebet	December/January
Shabatu	Shebat	January/February
Adaru I	Adar	February/March
Adaru II	Veadar	(intercalary)

Thus, the year in the Jewish (and Babylonian) calendar consists of 12 lunar months, with the addition of the intercalary month as necessary to synchronize with the solar year. The months contain alternately 29 or 30 days; the beginning of each is marked by the appearance of the new moon.

The Hebrew week ends with the observation of the Sabbath, lasting from sunset Friday to sunset Saturday, a day to rest and pay homage to God. The use of weeks and observation of a day of rest are primarily contributions from Jewish tradition to our present–day calendar. (See also **The Seven–day Week**, above.)

The Jewish Era, designated *A.M.* (for Latin *anno mundi*, "year of the world"), begins with the supposed date of Creation, which tradition sets at 3761 B.C. After more than two thousand years, devout Jews still observe essentially the same calendar for religious purposes, although they follow other calendars for their business and social lives. With its roots based in scripture, the Hebrew calendar has remained a primary binding force of tradition and continuity throughout the long and varied history of the Jewish people.

The Early Roman Calendar

Ancient Rome played a significant role in the development of our modern method of reckoning time. The earliest known Roman calendar, created according to legend by the city's founder, Romulus, in the eighth century B.C., had 10 months totaling 304 days: 6 months of 30 days and 4 months of 31 days. The new year began in March, the time when agricultural activities were revived and new military campaigns were initiated, and ended with December, which was followed by a winter gap that was used for intercalation. The Etruscan king Numa Pompilius (reigned 715–673 B.C.) reformed Romulus's primitive calendar, instituting a lunar year of 12 months. The two new months, following December, were named *Januarius* and *Februarius*, and were respectively assigned 29 and 28 days.

While this reform was a clear improvement, it was set aside in Rome during a time of political unrest that began about 510 B.C. Still, its advantages were remembered, and in 153 B.C. Numa Pompilius's calendar was again adopted. At the same time the beginning of the Roman civil year was changed to January 1, which became the day that newly elected consuls assumed office.

Days of the Roman Month

The Romans did not have a method for numbering the days of their months in a series. They did, however, establish three fixed points from which other days could be reckoned. These three designations were: 1) *Kalends*, the first day of the month (ancestor of English *calendar*); 2) *Nones*, the ninth day; and 3) *Ides*, originally the day of the full moon of the lunar month. In months of 31 days (March, May, July, October) the Nones were the seventh day and the Ides the fifteenth, while in the shorter months the Nones fell on the fifth and the Ides on the thirteenth day.

The Romans also recognized a market day, called *nundinae*, which occurred every eighth day. This established a cycle for agriculture in which the farmer worked for seven days in his field and brought his produce to the city on the eighth for sale.

The Julian Calendar

It was not until the mid-first century B.C., by which time the reformed lunar calendar had shifted eight weeks out of phase with the seasons, that emperor Julius Caesar determined that a long-term and scientific reform of the calendar must take place. He enlisted the aid of the Alexandrian astronomer Sosigenes to devise the new calendar. The solar year was reckoned quite accurately at 365.25, and the calendar provided for years of 365 days with an additional day in February every fourth year. In 46 B.C. a total of 90 days were intercalated into the year, bringing the calendar back into phase with the seasons. As a result, what would have been March 1, 45 B.C. was, in the new system, referred to as January 1, 45 B.C. Thus 46 B.C. was a long year, containing 445 days, and was referred to by Romans as *ultimus annus confusionis*, "the last year of the muddled reckoning."

In 10 B.C. it was found that the priests in charge of administering the new Roman calendar had wrongly intercalated the extra day every third year rather than every fourth. In order to rectify the situation, the emperor Augustus declared that no 366–day years should be observed for the next 12 years, and made certain that future intercalation would be properly conducted. With this minor adjustment, the Julian calendar was fully in place, so to remain for the next 1,626 years.

The Gregorian Calendar

Since the Julian calendar year of 365.25 days (averaging in the leap-year day) was slightly longer than the actual length of a solar year, 365.242199 days, over time even this system proved wanting, growing out of phase by about three or four days every four centuries. By the time of Pope Gregory XIII in the late sixteenth century, the difference between the calendar and the seasons had grown to ten days; the vernal equinox of 1582 occurred on March 11. Left without change, the Julian calendar would have resulted in fixed holy days occurring in the "wrong" season, which bewildered church officials. Moreover, certain fixed holy days were also used to determine when to plant and harvest crops.

Pope Gregory's reform, presented in the papal bull of February 24, 1582, consisted of deleting ten days from the year (the day following October 5 was designated as October 15) and declaring that three out of every four "century" years (1700, 1800, etc.) would not be leap years; if a century year, such as 1600, were divisible by 400, it would be a leap year. These modifications established the form of our present calendar.

In spite of its superior accuracy, the Gregorian calendar met with resistance in various parts of the world, and was not used until the eighteenth century in Protestant Europe and the American colonies, and even later still in areas under strong Byzantine influence.

Although the Gregorian calendar measures out a year that is slightly longer than the solar year (differing by about 25 seconds a year, or 3 days in every 10,000 years) its general workability and accuracy have led to its use worldwide for nearly all nonreligious purposes.

Calendar of Holidays

January

January 1
New Year's Day
Solemnity of Mary the Mother of God

January 1 or 2
St. Basil's Day

January 2
Second New Year

January 5–6
Epiphany Eve and Epiphany
Twelfth Night
Day of the Three Kings/Día de los Tres
Reyes

First Monday after Twelfth Day
Plough Monday

January 6 or 7
Old Christmas

January 7
Gannā
St. Distaff's Day
St. John the Baptist's Day

January 11
St. Brictiva's Day

January 12
Old New Year's Day

January 12–15
Festival of Our Lord Bonfim

January 13
St. Knut's Day
Old Silvester

January 14
Magh Sankranti

January 15
Pilgrimage to the Shrine of the Black
Christ
Adult's Day

January 16
St. Honoratus's Day

January 19 and 20
Timqat (Epiphany) and St. Michael's
Feast

January 20
St. Sebastian's Day
St. Agnes Eve

January 21
St. Sarkis's Day

January 22
St. Dominique's Day (Midwife's Day)
St. Vincent's Day

January 24
Festival of Abundance

January 25
Burns Night

Last Tuesday in January
Up Helly Aa

Fifteenth Day, Shevat (January–February)
Tu Bi-Shevat (Fifteenth Day, Shevat)

Month of Magha (January–February)
Urn Festival

Month of Tagu, Days 1–4
Thingyan

Last Month, Last Day of Lunar Year
New Year's Eve

Moon 1, Days 1–15
New Year

Moon 1, Day 1
Tibetan New Year (Losar)

Moon 1, First Two Weeks (circa February)
Prayer Festival

Moon 1, Day 7
Festival of the Seven Grasses

Moon 1, Day 9
Making Happiness Festival

Moon 1, Days 14–19 (circa February)
Butter Sculpture Offering Festival

Moon 1, Day 15
Great Fifteenth
Burning of the Moon House Festival
Lantern Festival
Birthday of the Great Emperor–Official
    of the Heavens

Moon 1, Day 16
Sixteenth Day

Moon 1, Day 19
Rats' Wedding Day

January–February
Rice Festival

Thai/Tai
Thai Poosam

February

Circa February
Tsagan Sara (New Year)

February
Clean Tent Ceremony
Winterlude

February 1
St. Brigid's Day

February 1–3 (circa)
Setsubun

February 2
Candlemas/Candelaria
Feast of the Virgin of the Suyapa
Queen of Waters Festival

February 3, 5
St. Blaise's Day, St. Agatha's Day

February 5
Igbi

February 10
Feast of St. Paul's Shipwreck

February 11
St. Vlasios's Day

February–March (Day 10 of Dhu'l-hija)
Id Al-Kabir (The Great Feast)

Moveable: February–March (Sunday before Lent)
Cheese Sunday

Moveable: February–March
Shrove Monday
Shrove Tuesday/Mardi Gras
Carnival
Ash Wednesday

Moveable: February–March (First Sunday in Lent)
Chalk Sunday

Moveable: February–April
Lent

February 14
St. Valentine's Day

Circa February 15–17
Igloo Festival

February 22
Boys' Day

February 25
St. George's Day

February 28
Feast of the Spring
Naked Festival

February 29
Leap Year Day/St. Oswald's Day

February (Full Moon)
Maka Buja

February–March (Full Moon)
Kason
Dol Purnima
Holi
Masi Magham

Pjalguna (February–March)
Sivaratri

Moon 2, Day 1 (February–March)
Wind Festival

February or March
Getting Out of the Water Festival (Kuomboko)

Moveable: February–March (Fourteenth Day of Adar)
Purim

March

First Two Weeks in March
Festival of the Water of Youth

March 1
First of March
St. David's Day

March 3
Hina Matsuri (Girls' Day)

Circa March 5
Feast of Excited Insects

March 8
Women's Day

March 9
Feast of the Forty Martyrs

Circa Mid-March, 1 Moons after Dosmoche
Storlog

March 17
St. Patrick's Day

March 19
St. Joseph's Day
Pookhyái

Circa March 20
Ibu Afo Festival
Emume Ala

Circa March 21
Vernal Equinox

Circa March 21 and Thirteen Days Thereafter
New Year

March 25
Day of the Annunciation

Moveable: March–April (Fourth Sunday in Lent)
Mothering Sunday

Moveable: March–April (Fifth Sunday in Lent)
Carlings Sunday

March–April (Saturday before Palm Sunday)
St. Lazarus's Day (Lazarovden)

March–April (Sunday before Easter)
Palm Sunday

Moveable: March 22–April 25
Easter and Holy Week

First Sunday after Easter (Low Sunday)
Domingo de Cuasimodo
St. Thomas's Day

Day after St. Thomas's Day (Low Sunday)
Blajini Day

Second Monday and Tuesday after Easter
Hocktide

Day 25 after Easter
Feast of Rousa

Day 28 after Easter
Ropotine

Moon 3, Day 5
Pure and Bright

Moon 3, Day 23
Birthday of Matsu

March–April
Gajan of Siva
Birthday of the Monkey God
Birthday of the Lord Vardhamana
Mahavira

March–April (Full Moon)
Panguni Uttiram

Day 9, Bright Fortnight, Chaitra (March–April)
Ramanavami

March–May
Flying Fish Ceremony

April

Circa April
Road Building Festival

April
Awuru Odo
Cherry Blossom Festival
New Year

April 1
April Fools' Day

April 2
13 Farvardin/Sizdeh Bedar

April 4
St. Isidore's Day

April 5 or 6 (105 Days after the Winter Solstice)
Pure Brightness Festival

Circa April (Eight Days Beginning on Day 15 of Nisan)
Pesach/Passover

Last Day of Passover and Day after Passover
Maimona

April 12 or 13
New Year

April 13–15
New Year

April 19–25 (The Thursday in This Period)
First Day of Summer

April 23
St. George's Day

April 25
St. Mark's Day

April 30
May Eve
Walpurgis Night

Moon 4, Day 8
Buddha's Birthday

April (Various Dates)
Planting Festivals
Wangkang Festival

April–May
First of Baisakh/Vaisakh

Full Moon (Purnima) of Vaisakha (April–May)
Buddha Jayanti

May

Circa May (Day 33 of the Omer Period)
Lag Ba-omer

May
Nongkrem Dance

May (Throughout the Month)
Flowers of May

First Sunday in May
Sunday School Day

First Tuesday in May
Fool's Fair

May 1
May Day
St. Joseph's Day

May 1–May 30
Birth of the Buffalo God

May 3
Day of the Holy Cross

May 5
Cinco de Mayo

May 5 (Formerly Moon 5, Day 5)
Boys' Day

Easter to July
Holy Ghost Season

Monday, Tuesday, and Wednesday before Ascension
Rogation Days

Moveable: Forty Days after Easter
Ascension Day

Moveable: Fifty Days after Easter
Whitsun/Pentecost

First Sunday after Whitsunday
Trinity

Moveable: Thursday after Trinity
Corpus Christi/Body of Christ

Seventh Thursday after Easter
Semik

First Thursday after Corpus Christi
Lajkonik

May 11–14
Ice Saints

May 14
Crossmas

May 15
St. Sofia's Day
St. Isidore's Day

May 17
Death of the Ground

May 24
Queen's Bithday (Victoria Day)

May 24–25
Pilgrimage of Sainte Sara

May 25
St. Urban's Day

May 29
Oak-Apple Day (Royal Oak Day)

May 31
Memorial Day (Day of the Dead)

May (Full Moon)
Wesak Day

Moon 5, Day 5 (May–June)
Double Fifth
Tano

Moon 5, Day 14
Gods of the Sea Festival (and Boat Race Day)

Moon 5, Day 15
Gogatsumatsuri

May–June
Sithinakha/Kumar Sasthi
Vata Savitri
Rocket Festival

May–June (Jaistha)
Ganga Dussehra

May–June (Day 6 of Sivan)
Shavuot

May to July (Height of Rainy Season)
Okere Juju

Circa May–July
Days 1–10 of Muharram

Late May or Early June
Star Snow (Qoyllur Rit'i)

June

Early June
Tyas Tuyï

June
Egungun Festival

June 1–2
Gawai Dayak

June 11
Cataclysmos Day

June 13
St. Anthony's Day

June 13–29
Festas Juninas

June 22–August 21
Aobao Gathering

June 24
St. John's Day/Midsumer Day
Day of the Indian

June 25
Festival of the Plow

June 27–July 27
Lesser New Year

June 29
Day of St. Peter and St. Paul

June or July (Rainy Season)
Car Festival (Rath Jatra)

Moon 8, Waning Day–Moon 11, Full Moon (June/July to September/October)
Vossa/Khao Vatsa/Waso

Moon 6, Day 6
Airing the Classics

Moon 6, Day 15
Shampoo Day (Yoodoonal)

Moon 6, Day 24
Birthday of the Lotus
Yi (China) New Year

May to October, Peaking in July
Festa Season

June–July or August–September
Pola and Hadaga

Late June to Early September
Powwow

July

Circa July
Olojo Festival (Ogun Festival)

Early July
Festival of the Ears of Grain

July
Nazareth Baptist Church Festival

July 1–2
Canada Day/Dominion Day

July 2 and August 16
Palio

July 4
Independence Day/Fourth of July

July 6
Feast of San Fermin

July 8
Feast of St. Elizabeth

July 11
Naadam Festival

July 14
Bastille Day

July 15
St. Swithin's Day
Festival of the Virgin of Carmen

July 25
St. James's Day

July 26
St. Anne's Day
Pardon of Ste. Ann d'Auray

July 29
St. Olaf's Wake

Moon 7, Day 7 (July–August)
Birthday of the Seven Old Maids
Star Festival/Double Seventh

Moon 7, Days 13–15 (July–August)
Obon

Moon 7, Day 15 (July–August)
Hungry Ghost Festival

July–August
Procession of Sacred Cows
Ghanta Karna
Kandy Esala Perahera
Marya
Snake Festival
Teej
Tish-Ah Be-Av

July–August (Full Moon)
Sacred Thread Festival

July or August
Maggomboh
Imechi Festival

Late July–First Tuesday of August
Carnival

Late July or Early August
Carnival

Full Moon in Summer
Tea Meetings

August

Early August
Llama Festival

August
Good Year Festival
Panchadaan

August 1
Feast of the Progress of the Precious
and Vivifying Cross
Honey Day
Lammas
Lúghnasa
Parents Day

August 2
Feast Day of Our Lady of the Angeles

August 2–7
Nebuta Festival

August 6
Transfiguration of Christ

August 10
Festival of St. Laurence

August 10–12
Puck's Fair

August 15
Assumption of the Virgin

August 20
St. Stephen's Fete

Circa August 24
Thanksgiving

August 30
La Rose

End of August
Reed Dance

August–September
Prachum Ben
Feast of the Dead
Festival of the Elephant God
Gokarna Aunsi

Plough Festival
Janmashtami
Lord Krishna's Birthday
Khordad-Sal
Paryushana
Agwunsi Festival
Insect-Hearing Festival

Moon 8, Day 15 (August–September)
Mid-Autumn Feast

Moon 8, Day 16 (August–September)
Birthday of the Monkey God

Various Dates
Harvest Festivals

September

Circa September
Okpesi Festival

September
Indra Jatra

September 8
Nativity of the Virgin

First and Second Days of Tishri (September–October)
Rosh Hashana

September 11
Coptic New Year
Enkutatash (New Year)

September 14
Holy Cross Day

September 15
Keiro no Hi (Respect for the Elderly Day)

Tenth Day of Tishri
Yom Kippur

12 Rabi-ul Awal (August–October)
Ma-ulid

Circa September 21–22
Autumnal Equinox
Jūgowa

September 27
Maskal

September 29
St. Michael's Day

Fifth Day of the Fifth Lunar Month (Late September–Early October)
Bon Kate

Moon 9, Day 9 (September–October)
Double Ninth
Chrysanthemum Day
Festival of the Nine Imperial Gods

Month 10 (September–October)
Ho Khao Slak

Days 24 and 25 of Tishri (September–October)
Simhat Torah and Is'ru Chag

September–October
Durga Puja/Dasain/Dussehra/Durgotsava
Oktoberfest
Pitra Visarjana Amavasya

October

Circa October (Wagyut Moon, Day 15)
Ok Pansa/Ok Vatsa/Thadingyut

October
Lord of the Earthquake

First Sunday in October
St. Michael's Day
Water Festival

Second Sunday in October
Lotu-A-Tamaiti

October 5
Han'gul Day

October 7
Festival of the Virgin of Rosario

October 17
Romería of Our Lady of Valme

October 18
St. Luke's Day

October 21
Festival of the Black Christ

October 25
St. Crispin and St. Crispinian's Day

October 26
St. Demetrius's Day

October 28
Thanksgiving
Punkie Night

October 31
All Hallow's Eve/All Saints' Eve

Moon 10, Day 1 (October–November)
Sending the Winter Dress

Moon 10, Day 25 (October–November)
Sang-joe

Kartik (October–November)
Gopashtami ("Cow Eighth") and
Govardhan Puja

October–November
Diwali/Deepavali/Tihar
Karwachoth

**Seven Days, Beginning Fifteenth of Tishri
(October–November)**
Sukkot

**Moveable: October or Later (after Rainy
Season)**
Mother's Day

November

Late Autumn
Keretkun Festival

Circa November
Seal Festival
Loi Krathong

Early November (Near End of Rainy Season)
Sango Festival

November
Tori-no-inchi

November 1
All Saints' Day

November 2
All Souls' Day

Friday before November 3
Creole Day

November 3
St. Hubert's Day

November 5
Guy Fawkes Night

**Twenty-seventh Day of Rajab (November 6
in 1999)**
Night of the Ascension

November 8
St. Michael's Day

November 11
St. Martin's Day
St. Mennas's Day

November 15
Shichi-go-san (Seven-Five-Three)

Circa November 15
Haile Selassie's Coronation Day

November 18
Feast of St. Plato the Martyr

November 19
Settlement Day

November 21
Presentation of the Virgin Mary in the
Temple

November 25
St. Catherine's Day

Fourth Thursday in November
Thanksgiving

November 30
St. Andrew's Day

Moon 8, Day 29 (November)
Seged

Month 12 (November)
Boun Phan Vet

Moveable: Month of Shaban
Shaban

Moveable: November–December
Ramadan (Month of Fasting)

December

Circa December (Tasaungmon Full Moon)
Tawadeintha/Tazaungdaing

Sunday before Advent (Early December)
Stir-Up Sunday

Four Weeks before Christmas, Beginning on a Sunday
Advent Season

Early December (Variable)
Bear Festival

Circa December (Eight Days Beginning on 25 Kislev)
Hanukkah

December 4
St. Barbara's Day

December 6
St. Nicholas's Day

December 7
Burning the Devil

Circa December 7–8
Itul

December 8
Immaculate Conception
Needle Day

Second Sunday before Christmas
Mother's Day

December 12
Our Lady of Guadalupe

December 13
St. Lucy's Day

December 14
St. Spiridion Day

December 16
Braaiveleis

December 16–25
Cock Crow Mass

Sunday before Christmas
Father's Day

Friday before Christmas
Cuci Negeri

December 18
St. Modesto's Day

Circa December 21
Ysyakh

December 21
St. Thomas's Day

Circa December 22
Winter Solstice

December 23
Festival of St. Naum
St. Thorlak's Day
La Noche de Rabanos (Night of the Radishes)

December 25–30 (Variable)
Kushi Festival

December 25
Christmas

December 26
Boxing Day
Kwanzaa
St. Stephen's Day

December 27
St. John's Day

December 28
Holy Innocents' Day

December 31
New Year's Eve
Sylvester Day

Late December
Sing-Sing

Moon 12, Day 8 (December–January)
Rice Cake Festival

Moon 12, Day 20 (December–January)
Day for Sweeping Floors

Moon 12, Day 23 or 24 (December–January)
Kitchen God Visits Heaven

Moon 12, Day 28 (December–January)
King's New Year

December–January
Little Feast

December–August
Odo

Words to Know

A

Absolute monarchy: A form of government in which a king or queen has absolute control over the people, who have no voice in their government.

Act of merit: An act of charity that, in Buddhism, is said to help the doer find favor with Buddha and earn credits toward a good rebirth.

Advent: A Christian holiday. From the Latin *adventus,* "coming," referring to the birth of Jesus. Advent is a four-week period of preparation for Christmas, beginning on the Sunday nearest November 30.

Age of Enlightenment: A philosophical movement during the eighteenth century when European writers, journalists, and philosophers influenced thousands through new ideas about an individual's right to determine his or her own destiny in life, including having a voice in government. The movement emphasized the use of reason to challenge previously accepted church teachings and traditions and thus is sometimes referred to as the Age of Reason.

Aliyah: From the Hebrew for "ascent" or "going up." The waves of Jewish immigrants to Israel in the nineteenth and twentieth centuries.

Allah: The "one God" of Islam.

Ancestors: A person's, tribe's, or cultural group's forefathers or recently deceased relatives.

Asceticism: A way of life marked by severe self-denial as a form of personal and spiritual discipline; for example, depriving the body of food and owning few material goods.

Ash Wednesday: A Christian holiday. Ash Wednesday is the seventh Wednesday before Easter and the first day of Lent, a season of fasting commemorating Jesus Christ's forty days of temptation in the wilderness. The name is derived from the practice of priests placing ashes on the foreheads of worshipers as a remembrance "that you are dust and unto dust you shall return."

B

Bastille: A castle and fortress in Paris, France, built in 1370 and later used as a prison. Bastille Day commemorates the storming of the Bastille by French peasants and workers on July 14, 1789, sparking the French Revolution.

Bee: A large gathering, usually of farm families, to complete a task and celebrate with food and drink, games, and dancing.

Beignet: A square fritter without a hole that is a popular snack during Carnival in France and French-influenced New Orleans, Louisiana. Fried pastries are popular throughout the world during Carnival, a time when people traditionally tried to use up their butter and animal fat before the Christian holiday of Lent.

Black Madonna: Poland's most famous religious icon, a painting of the Virgin Mary holding the infant Jesus, said to have been painted by Saint Luke during the first century A.D.

Blessing baskets: Baskets of Easter foods and pysanky (Easter eggs), covered with hand-embroidered cloths and carried to church to be blessed on Holy Saturday in Ukraine and Poland.

Bodhi tree: The "tree of wisdom." Buddha achieved enlightenment while sitting under a bodhi tree.

Bourgeoisie: In French, the middle social class.

Buddha: Prince Siddhartha Gautama (c. 563–c. 483 B.C.) of India, later given the name Buddha ("the Enlightened One"). His teachings became the foundation of Buddhism.

Buddhism: One of the major religions of Asia and one of the five largest religious systems in the world. Buddhists believe that suffering is an inescapable part of life and that peace can be achieved only by practicing charity, temperance, justice, honesty, and truth. They also believe in a continual cycle of birth, illness, death, and rebirth.

Byzantine Empire: The Eastern Roman Empire, with its capital at Constantinople (present-day Istanbul, Turkey).

C

Cajun: The name given to French Canadians who emigrated from Acadia, a former name for Nova Scotia. The name was eventually shortened from "Acadian" to "Cajun."

Calligraphy: Ornamental handwriting. In Islam, it is the Arabic script in which the Koran is written and which is used inside mosques as an art form.

Calypso: A popular musical style originating in Trinidad and Tobago in which singers create witty lyrics to a particular rhythm.

Carnavalesco: An individual who helps design, plan, and choreograph Carnival parades and shows in Brazil.

Caste system: A social system in which people are divided into classes according to their skin color and ancestry.

Catholic Church: The ancient undivided Christian church or a church claiming historical continuity from it.

Celts: A people who lived in Ireland, Scotland, England, Wales, and northern France before the birth of Christ, more than two thousand years ago. Also refers to modern people of these areas.

Chinese zodiac: A zodiac system based on a twelve-year cycle, with each year named after one of twelve animals. A person's zodiac sign is the animal representing the year in which he or she was born.

Christian Protestantism: Christian church denominations that reject certain aspects of Catholicism and Orthodox Christianity and believe in salvation by faith alone, the Holy Bible as the only source of God's revealed truth, and the "priesthood" of all believers.

Civil disobedience: Nonviolent action, such as protest marches, taken by an individual or group in an attempt to bring about social change.

Civil rights: Rights granted to every member of a society regardless of race, sex, age, creed, or religious beliefs. Specifically, the rights given by certain amendments to the U.S. Constitution.

Collective farm: A large farm, especially in former communist countries, formed by combining many small farms for joint operation under government control.

Colonial rule: A country's rule of a foreign land that has settlers from the ruling country, or colonists, living there.

Commedia dell'arte: Italian comedy of the sixteenth to eighteenth centuries that created some of the most famous characters in Italian costume. Among them are Harlequin, with his multicolored suit, and Punchinello, who later became a famous character in puppet shows.

Communism: A political and economic system in which the government controls and owns the means of production of goods and distributes the goods equally among the population.

Concentration camps: Nazi German military camps where civilians, primarily Jews, were held during World War II (1939–45). Millions were tortured, gassed, or burned to death in these camps.

Constitutional monarchy: A form of government in which a nation is ruled by a king or queen but the people are represented through executive, legislative, and judicial branches.

Continental Congress: Men representing twelve of the thirteen American colonies (all but Georgia) who formed a colonial government in 1774 in Philadelphia, Pennsylvania, and set forth the principles of the American Revolution (1775–83).

Cornucopia: A horn-shaped basket overflowing with vegetables and fruits. The cornucopia is a symbol of a bountiful harvest, often used as a Thanksgiving decoration. Also called "horn of plenty."

Council of Nicaea: In 325, a church governing body led by Roman emperor Constantine (reigned 306–37) met in the city of Nicaea (in what is now Turkey). The council formally established the Feast of Christ's Resurrection (Easter) and decreed that it should be celebrated on the Sunday following the first full moon after the spring equinox.

Coup d'état: A military takeover of an existing government.

Crazy days: In many European countries, the final days of Carnival celebrations, the wildest and most widely celebrated.

Creole: A person descended from or culturally related to early French or sometimes Spanish settlers of the U.S. Gulf Coast; they preserve a characteristic form of French speech and culture.

Crucifixion: A Roman method of execution, in which a person is nailed to a wooden cross to die.

Crusades: Religious wars of the eleventh, twelfth, and thirteenth centuries in which Christians fought to win the Holy Land from the Muslims.

D

Dedication: The setting apart of a temple or church for sacred uses with solemn rites.

Dharma: Laws of nature that were taught by Buddha. The primary symbol of Buddhism is a wheel with eight spokes, called the dharma wheel, which symbolizes life's constant cycles of change and the Eightfold Path to enlightenment.

Diaspora: The breaking up and scattering of a people from their homeland, especially the scattering of the Jewish people from Israel throughout the world.

Divination: Predicting the future through ritual; fortune-telling.

Dragon parade: A Chinese New Year parade featuring long dragon costumes manipulated by many dancers.

Dreidel: A four-sided top, each side marked with a Hebrew letter, all together representing the phrase "A great miracle happened there," referring to the Hanukkah miracle in ancient Jerusalem. The term also refers to the Hanukkah game played by Jewish children with the top.

Druids: An order of Celtic priests.

E

Easter bunny: Originally the Easter hare, called "Oschter Haws" by the Germans; a mythical rabbit who is said to bring colored eggs and candy to children on Easter Sunday.

Easter egg: An egg colored or decorated for Easter.

Easter lily: The white trumpet lily, native to Bermuda but widely cultivated in the United States. It blooms at Easter time and is known as a symbol of purity and of Christ's Resurrection.

Eastern Orthodox Church: A branch of the Christian church with many members in Eastern Europe, Western Asia, and the Mediterranean. The Eastern Orthodox Church began in the Greek city of Constantinople (now Istanbul, Turkey), the seat of

Roman emperor Constantine's (reigned 306–37) Eastern Roman Empire.

Elders: Older family or community members, such as grandparents, who are honored and respected for their experience and wisdom.

Enlightenment: Understanding the truth about human existence; a spiritual state marked by the absence of desire or suffering, upon which Buddhist teaching is based.

Epiphany of Our Lord: A Christian holiday. Traditionally observed on January 6, Epiphany marks the official end of the Christmas season. In Western Christian churches, Epiphany commemorates the visit of the Three Wise Men to see the infant Jesus in Bethlehem; in Eastern Orthodox churches, it is celebrated as the day of Jesus' baptism.

Epitaphion: A carved structure covered with a gold-embroidered cloth and decorated with flowers that is a symbol of Christ's tomb in the Greek Orthodox Church.

Epitaphios: "Feast of Sorrow." A Good Friday ritual in the Greek Orthodox Church, enacted as a funeral procession for Jesus Christ.

Equinox: The first day of spring and the first day of fall of each year, when the length of the day's sunlight is equal to the length of the day's darkness. This occurs on about March 20 or 21 and September 22 or 23.

Essence: The "spirit" of a thing, such as food or burnt offerings, which is believed to be usable by the dead in many cultures.

F

Fantasia: "Fantasy." Brazilian name for Carnival costume.

Fast: To voluntarily go without food or drink, often as part of religious practice, as during Ramadan or Lent.

Feudal system: The predominant economic and social structure in Europe from about the ninth to the fifteenth centuries, in which peasants farmed land for nobles and in turn received a small house and plot of land for themselves.

First fruits: The first harvesting of a crop, considered sacred by many cultures.

Folk holiday: A nonreligious holiday that originates with the common people.

Fool societies: In Germany and other parts of Europe, guilds formed by tradesmen to plan and organize Carnival celebrations.

Four Noble Truths: The four principles that became the core of Buddha's teaching: 1) Suffering is everywhere; 2) The cause of suffering is the attempt to satisfy selfish desires; 3) Suffering can be stopped by overcoming selfish desires; and 4) The way to end craving and suffering is to follow the Eightfold Path, eight steps concerning the right way to think and conduct oneself.

Freedom of the press: The right of people to publish and distribute pamphlets, newspapers, and journals containing their own thoughts and observations without censorship by government or church.

French Quarter: A historical section of New Orleans, Louisiana, where the wildest and most elaborate Mardi Gras celebrations are staged.

G

Gelt: The traditional Jewish name for money given to the poor during Hanukkah. Also refers to any Hanukkah gift and to play money (chocolate coins wrapped in gold foil) used in playing dreidel.

Gilles: A special men's society in Belgium whose members dress in identical costumes and masks and march in Mardi Gras parades.

Golden Stool of the Ashanti: A wooden stool covered with a layer of gold. The stool is sacred to the Ashanti people of Ghana, to whom it is a symbol of their nation and their king.

Good Friday: The Friday before Easter Sunday, a day for mourning Christ's death.

Gregorian calendar: The calendar in general use in much of the world in modern times. It was introduced by Pope Gregory XIII in 1582 as a modification of the Roman Julian calendar.

Griot: A storyteller who passes on the history of a people orally and through music.

Guerrilla: A member of a small military organization that uses unconventional fighting tactics to surprise and ambush their enemies.

Guillotine: A machine for beheading criminals, widely used by French revolutionaries during the late 1700s and for many years afterward in France. It consisted of a wooden frame with a heavy, tapered blade hoisted to the top and then dropped, immediately severing the victim's head.

Guising: An old Scottish custom of dressing in disguise and going from house to house asking for treats; a forerunner of Halloween trick-or-treating.

H

Hanukkiah: A Hanukkah menorah, or candleholder. It has eight main branches and a ninth for the servant candle, used to light the other eight.

Harvest festival: A festival for celebrating the gathering of crops at the end of the growing season.

Harvest moon: The full moon nearest to the time of the fall equinox (about September 23), so called because it occurs at the traditional time of harvest in the Northern Hemisphere. It appears larger and brighter than the usual full moon, and the moon is full for an extra night, giving farmers more hours to harvest crops.

Hegira: The flight of Muhammad and his followers in 622 from Mecca to Yathrib, later known as Medina, where Muhammad was accepted as a prophet. The Hegira marks the beginning of the Islamic calendar.

Hidalgo's bell: A cathedral bell rung by Father Miguel Hidalgo y Costilla in the town of Dolores on September 16, 1810, to call the native people of Mexico together in a revolt against Spanish rule.

Hinduism: The major religion of India and one of the world's oldest religions. It is based on the natural laws of dharma and conforming to one's duty through ritual, social observances, and meditation.

Holocaust: The mass slaughter by the Nazis of some six million Jews and thousands of other European civilians during World War II (1939–45), chiefly by gassing and burning the victims.

Holy Communion: A church rite in which Christians eat and drink blessed bread and wine as memorials of Christ's death. Christ is said to have initiated the rite during the Last Supper.

Holy Grail: A cup or plate that, according to medieval legend, Jesus used at the Last Supper.

Holy Land: Palestine, where Jesus Christ lived, preached, died, and was resurrected, according to the Bible. Major holy sites are Jerusalem and Bethlehem.

Holy Shroud: In the Orthodox Church in Ukraine, a specially woven and embroidered cloth that represents Jesus' burial cloth, used for Holy Week services.

I

Icons: Religious scenes or figures such as Christ and the Virgin Mary, usually very old, painted on wooden panels or on linen or cotton cloth glued to panels. Revered by Christians in the Eastern Orthodox and Catholic Churches, some are believed to have miraculous powers.

Iftar: The nighttime feast served after sunset during Ramadan.

Imam: Person who leads prayer and recites from the Koran during worship services in a mosque.

Immigrants: People who leave their home country and enter another to settle.

Islam: The major religion of the Middle East, northern Africa, parts of Southeast Asia, and some former Soviet Union countries. Islam is the world's second-largest religion. Believers, called Muslims, worship their one god, Allah, and assert that Muhammad (c. 570–632), founder of Islam, is his prophet.

Islamic calendar: The lunar calendar used to determine the date of Islamic holidays. Each of twelve months begins with the first sighting of the new moon. Each lunar month has either twenty-nine or thirty days, and each year has 354 days.

J

Jataka Tales: A collection of more than five-hundred tales said to have been told by Buddha. The tales were passed down orally through generations and finally written down several hundred years after his death. About Buddha's previous lives, the tales concern such issues as responsibility, friendship, honesty, ecology, and respect for elders.

Jesus Christ: The founder of Christianity. Jesus was born in Bethlehem in about 6 B.C. and died in about A.D. 30, when he was crucified. According to Christian tradition,

Jesus was the Son of God, and he came into the world to die for the sins of mankind. His followers believe that as Christ rose from the dead and ascended into heaven, so too will they.

Julian calendar: The calendar introduced in Rome in 46 B.C. and on which the modern-day Gregorian calendar is based.

K

Kitchen God: A Chinese deity honored during the lunar New Year. He is said to reside in the kitchen and report to the Jade Emperor (the highest deity, who resides in heaven) once a year on the actions of each household.

Koran: The Islamic holy book, written in Arabic and containing Scriptures also found in the Jewish Torah and the Christian Bible, as well as rules on all aspects of human living. The Koran is believed to have been revealed to the prophet Muhammad by Allah through the angel Gabriel.

Krewes: Secretive, members-only clubs that organize Mardi Gras parades and activities in New Orleans, Louisiana.

L

Lakshmi: The Hindu goddess of wealth, honored during Diwali, the Hindu New Year.

Last Supper: Also called the Lord's Supper; the last meal Jesus Christ shared with his disciples, believed to have been a Passover meal and at which Christ is said to have initiated the rite of Holy Communion. Christians observe the Thursday before Easter in memory of the Last Supper.

Legal holiday: A day declared an official holiday by a government, meaning that government offices, schools, and usually banks and other offices are closed so that workers may observe the holiday.

Lent: A Christian holiday. Lent is the traditional six-week period of partial fasting that precedes Easter. It is a time to remember the forty days that Jesus wandered in the desert without food. Many Christians give up a favorite food or activity during Lent.

Lunar New Year: A movable holiday marking the first day of the first lunar month on the Chinese lunar calendar. It begins at sunset on the day of the second new moon following the winter solstice (between late January and the end of February) and ends on the fifteenth day of the first lunar month.

M

Mardi Gras: *See* Shrove Tuesday.

Martyr: One who voluntarily suffers death for proclaiming his or her religious beliefs and refusing to give them up.

Masked ball: A formal dance at which those attending wear costumes and masks that conceal their identity.

Mass: A celebration of the Christian sacrament of the Eucharist (Holy Communion), commemorating the sacrifice of the body and blood of Christ, symbolized by consecrated bread and wine.

Maundy Thursday: The Thursday before Easter Sunday, said to be the day Christ took the Last Supper, prayed in the Garden of Gethsemane, was betrayed by Judas Iscariot, and was arrested. In many churches, this is a day for taking Holy Communion in memory of the Last Supper.

Mecca: The holiest city of Islam. It is located in Saudi Arabia and is the birthplace of the prophet Muhammad. Muslims strive to make a pilgrimage to Mecca at least once during their lifetime and face toward Mecca each time they pray.

Menorah: A seven-pronged candleholder used in Jewish worship ceremonies.

Messiah: The "anointed," the Savior prophesied in the Bible to save the world from sin. To Christians, the Messiah is Jesus Christ.

Metta: One of Buddha's main teachings, involving the concept of loving kindness. Metta is a way to overcome anger through love, evil through good, and untruth through truth.

Middle Path: A major tenant of Buddhism advocating equilibrium (balance) between extremes in life and avoiding things or ideas produced by selfish desires. Buddhists believe the best way to travel the Middle Path is through meditation, as Buddha did.

Mishnah: The Jewish code of law, passed down orally for centuries before being written down by rabbis during the second century.

Missionaries: People sent to other countries to teach their religious beliefs to native peoples and carry on humanitarian work.

Monk: A man who is a member of a religious order and usually lives in a monastery or wanders from place to place teaching religious principles.

Monsoon: The name give to a season of heavy rains and wind in India and southern Asia.

Mosque: An Islamic temple for prayer and worship, consisting of a large dome and at least one pointed tower, or minaret. Mosques are decorated with calligraphy from the Koran.

Movable holiday: A holiday that falls at a different time each year, depending on the calendar used to determine the celebration. For example, Thanksgiving, Ramadan, and Easter.

Muhammad: Islam's greatest prophet. Muhammad was an Arabian who lived during the sixth century (c. 570–632). He is considered the founder of Islam.

Mumming: Merrymaking in disguise during festivals.

Muslim: A follower of the Islamic faith.

N

Nativity: The birth of Jesus Christ, as told in the biblical New Testament.

Nazarenos: Honorable men who lead Holy Week processions in Spain, wearing long robes and pointed hoods that cover their faces.

New moon: The thin crescent moon that appears after sunset following nights during the beginning of the new moon phase, when no moon can be seen. The new moon is used to mark the beginning of each month in both the Islamic and Jewish calendars.

Night of Power: The twenty-seventh night of Ramadan, which Muslims believe is the night when the angel Gabriel first began giving the words of the Koran to the prophet Muhammad.

Nirvana: A state of perfect peace and joy; freedom from greed, anger, and sorrow.

Nun: A woman who is a member of a religious order.

O

Ofrenda: Spanish word for an offering made to the dead or to a religious figure.

Oratorio: A long choral music piece for many voices, without action or scenery, usually on a religious theme. For example, Handel's *Messiah*.

P

Pagan: Referring to the worship of many gods, especially to early peoples who worshiped gods of nature.

Palm Sunday: The Sunday before Easter, when Jesus' entry into Jerusalem is commemorated with palms, which were used to line his path.

Papier-mâché: A mixture of flour, paper, paste, and water that hardens when dry and is often used to create figures and objects for Carnival parade floats and for many other craft projects.

Parade float: A large platform that is elaborately decorated and carries people and scenery representing a specific parade theme. Floats are usually mounted on a trailer and pulled through the streets by a motor vehicle. Float design and building is often considered an art.

Parol: A traditional Filipino symbol of Christmas, a star-shaped lantern made from bamboo and paper, called the Star of Bethlehem.

Paschal candle: A large candle, sometimes weighing hundreds of pounds, that is lit in some churches on Holy Saturday and used to light many individual candles for congregation members. The Paschal candle represents Christ as the light of the world.

Passion of Jesus Christ: The sufferings that Christ endured between the night of the Last Supper with his disciples and his death by crucifixion, often reenacted by Christians during Holy Week.

Passion play: A dramatic musical play reenacting Christ's Passion and crucifixion.

Passover: An observance of the Jews' deliverance from slavery in Egypt, as told in the Bible. Jewish families were commanded to smear the blood of a sacrificial lamb on their doorways so that the angel of death would pass over their homes. Passover is still a major Jewish observance. Christians also commemorate Passover by taking Holy Communion on Maundy Thursday, the day Christ is said to have eaten a Passover meal with his disciples at the Last Supper.

Patron saint: A saint believed to represent and protect a group of people, church, nation, city or town, animals, or objects. A saint to whom people pray for help in certain circumstances.

Penitents: In Holy Week processions in Spain, the Philippines, and Central and South America, persons who walk in the procession carrying heavy wooden crosses, in chains, or whipping themselves as punishment and repentance for wrongs they have done and to commemorate Christ's suffering as he carried the Cross.

Pilgrimage: A journey, usually to a holy place or shrine.

Pilgrims: Name given to English colonists who arrived at what is now Plymouth, Massachusetts, in 1621 and settled there. This group is credited with celebrating the first Thanksgiving, with members of the Wampanoag Indian tribe.

Pongol: A sweet, boiled rice dish that is prepared to celebrate the rice harvest in parts of India. Pongol is also the name given to this holiday.

Pope: A high-ranking bishop who is head of the Roman Catholic Church and resides in the Vatican in Rome.

Proclamation: An official formal public announcement, usually by a government leader or representative.

Promised Land: According to the biblical book of Genesis, the land of Canaan, promised by God to Abraham, the father of the Jews. The prophet Moses led the Hebrews to the Promised Land after freeing them from slavery in Egypt. Refers to modern-day Israel.

Prophet: One who speaks for God or a deity; a divinely inspired speaker, interpreter, or spokesperson who passes on to the people things revealed to him or her by God.

Proverb: A wise saying or adage, often part of the cultural heritage of a people.

Puritans: Members of a sixteenth- and seventeenth-century religious Protestant group in England and New England that believed in a strict work ethic and opposed ceremony and celebration.

Pysanky: Ukrainian and Polish Easter eggs created by using the wax resist, or batik, method.

R

Rabbi: A Jewish religious teacher and leader.

Reincarnation: A Hindu belief that all life is part of a universal creative force called Brahman and that human and animal souls are reborn into new bodies many times before they return to Brahman.

Resurrection of Jesus Christ: The rising from the dead of Jesus Christ, the central figure of Christianity, worshiped as the son of God. The Resurrection is celebrated at Easter. Christians believe that Christ died to reconcile humans with God and that believers will have eternal life of the spirit.

S

Sabzeh: A dish of sprouts grown by Iranian families in preparation for Nouruz, the New Year celebration. The sprouts are said to absorb bad luck from the past year.

Saint: A person, usually deceased, who has been officially recognized by church officials as holy because of deeds performed during his or her lifetime.

Samba: A fast dance made famous in Rio de Janeiro, Brazil, in which the feet and hips move but the upper body is kept still. The samba is performed by large groups of dancers, called samba schools, who wear elaborate matching costumes in Carnival parades.

Samhain: An annual festival of the Celts that marked the end of the fall harvest and the beginning of winter. It is said to be the forerunner of Halloween and New Year celebrations in parts of Europe.

Sangha: A Buddhist community of monks and nuns.

Secular: Nonreligious.

Seven Principles of Kwanzaa: A set of principles developed for Kwanzaa laying out rules of living for the community of people of African descent: unity, self-determination, collective work and responsibility, cooperative economics, purpose, creativity, and faith.

Shofar: An ancient Jewish traditional trumpet-like instrument made from a ram's or antelope's horn that is blown in the synagogue during Rosh Hashanah and Yom Kippur.

Shrine: A place, either natural or manmade, set aside for worship of a god or saint; a box or structure containing religious relics or images.

Shrove Tuesday: The Tuesday before Ash Wednesday, also called Fat Tuesday (Mardi Gras in French). Shrove Tuesday is the final day of Carnival and the one on which the biggest celebrations are held. Traditionally a time for confessing sins (called "being shriven") and for using up the fresh meat and animal fat, eggs, and butter in the household before the forty-day fast of Lent.

Solstice: The first day of summer and the first day of winter in the northern hemisphere, when daylight hours are the longest and shortest, respectively. The solstices fall about June 22 and December 22 of each year.

Spring couplets: Two-line rhymes written in Chinese calligraphy that are displayed during Chinese New Year as a wish for good luck.

Star of David: A six-pointed star believed to have decorated the shield of King David of Israel, who ruled about 1000 B.C. A widely used symbol of Judaism.

Stations of the Cross: The locations in Jerusalem and the corresponding events leading to the Crucifixion and Resurrection of Christ. A central theme of Christian religious art and sculpture, Holy Week processions, and Passion plays.

Steel drum: A drum created in Trinidad and Tobago, originally by using discarded steel oil barrels. Steel drum bands and music have become popular worldwide.

Suhur: The pre-dawn meal served each morning of Ramadan.

Supernatural: Transcending the laws of nature; referring to ghosts and spirits and the spiritual realm.

Superstition: A belief that something will happen or not happen as a result of performing a specific ritual, for example, eating certain foods to bring good luck.

Swahili: A major African language. Many of the terms relating to Kwanzaa are drawn from Swahili.

Synagogue: A Jewish house of worship.

T

Tableau: A group of people in costume creating a living picture or scene portraying a historical, mythological, musical, or narrative theme.

Taboo: Something forbidden by religious or cultural rules, sometimes because of the fear of punishment by supernatural powers.

Talmud: The authoritative book of Jewish tradition, consisting of the Mishnah and

the Gemara, comments of rabbis about the Mishnah.

Tamboradas: Loud, steady drumbeats that sound in many Spanish cities and villages beginning at midnight on Holy Thursday and continuing until late on Holy Saturday night, announcing the Passion and death of Christ.

Throws: Objects such as plastic bead necklaces and coins, flowers, candy, or fruit thrown to the crowd from parade floats or by marching groups, especially in Carnival parades.

Torah: The Jewish holy book, consisting of the five books of Moses (first five books of the biblical Old Testament), also called the Pentateuch.

Trick-or-treating: A widely popular Halloween tradition for children in which they dress in costumes and go from door to door collecting candy and treats. Children once played tricks on those who did not give treats.

V

Vaya: A sprig of bay or myrtle attached to a small cross made from a palm frond, given by Greek Orthodox priests to members of their congregation on Palm Sunday.

Vegetarian: Eating no meat, and sometimes no animal products, such as dairy foods or eggs.

Viceroy: The governor of a country or territory who rules in the name of a king or queen.

Virgin of Guadalupe: The Virgin Mary, mother of Jesus Christ, as she is said to have appeared (with dark skin and Mexican Indian clothing) to an Indian woodcutter in 1531. She is the patron saint of Mexico's poor.

W

Witch: A woman accused of worshiping Satan and casting spells to help him do evil to humans. Witches are often fictitious characters and the subject of Halloween costumes.

Y

Yule log: A large log burned in a fireplace during the Christmas season, a custom that began in early Europe and Scandinavia.

Z

Zakat: Money given by Muslims to help the poor in obedience to the laws of Islam and as a means of worshiping Allah.

Zion: The name of a fortification in the ancient city of Jerusalem, capital of King David's kingdom in about 1000 B.C. For centuries, Zion has been a symbol of the Promised Land (Israel) and of Judaism.

Zionism: A movement to rebuild the Jewish state in Israel; from the word Zion, another name for Jerusalem.

Zoroastrianism: The ancient religion of Persia, developed by the prophet Zoroaster (c. 628–551 B.C.). Believers perform good deeds to help the highest deity, Ahura Mazda, battle the evil spirit Ahriman.

Junior
Worldmark
Encyclopedia of

World Holidays

Buddha's Birthday

Also Known As:
Visakha Puja
Buddha Day
Hana Matsuri (Flower Festival)
Feast of the Lanterns

Introduction

Buddhism (pronounced BOO-dih-zem) is one of the major religions of Asia and is one of the five largest in the world. It was founded by Prince Siddhartha Gautama (pronounced sid-DAR-tuh GOW-tuh-muh; c. 563–c. 483 B.C.), who was later given the name Buddha, meaning "the Enlightened One" or "the One Who Has Awakened." Buddha's birthday is celebrated by millions of people in Thailand, Vietnam, Korea, Cambodia, Tibet, China, Japan, and elsewhere in Asia. It is also celebrated in Europe, the United States, and other countries in the West.

In Thailand and other countries where Theravada Buddhism (pronounced THER-uh-VAH-duh; the oldest and most conservative branch of the religion) is practiced, Visakha Puja (pronounced vie-SOCK-uh POO-jah) commemorates not only Buddha's birthday but also two other important events in his life: his attainment of enlightenment (spiritual knowledge) and his death. Buddha's birthday is celebrated on the day of the full moon of May. Buddhists believe Buddha attained enlightenment exactly thirty-five years later on the same date, and that he died on the same date at the age of eighty.

After his enlightenment, Buddha spent the next forty-five years before his death teaching others what he had learned about the natural laws of human existence and how individuals could escape the suffering found in this world. His teachings are one of "the Three Jewels," also known as "the Three Refuges" or "the Three Treasures," which summarize Buddhist belief. Buddhists invoke the Three Jewels every day: "I take refuge in the Buddha. I take refuge in the *dharma* (Buddha's teachings). I take refuge in the *sangha* (the community of monks and nuns)."

History

Some twenty-five hundred years ago, around 563 B.C., on the day of the full moon of May, a son was born to the king and queen of a small Indian kingdom in the foothills of the Himalayas, a mountain range in northeastern India. He was born in Lumbini, which today is part of Nepal and located just across the border from India. His name was Siddhartha Gautama.

Holiday Fact Box: Buddha's Birthday

Themes

On this day, Theravada Buddhists in Thailand, Southeast Asia, and around the world celebrate Buddha's birth; his attainment of enlightenment (spiritual knowledge), upon which Buddhist teaching is based; and his death, all of which are said to have occurred on the same day of the year.

Type of Holiday

Buddha's birthday is a religious holiday, one of the three moon festivals celebrated by Buddhists. It is the holiest day of the Buddhist year.

When Celebrated

In most Buddhist countries in southeastern Asia, Buddha's birthday is celebrated on the full-moon day of the month of Visakha, usually May. In other Buddhist countries, including Vietnam, China, Japan, and Korea, Buddha's birth—but not his enlightenment or death—is celebrated on April 8.

Because of a prophecy at the time of his birth that Siddhartha would grow up to be either a great king or, if he saw suffering, a great holy man, his father was determined to keep him on the path to royalty. He guarded him from ugliness and suffering and provided him with a life of luxury. He gave Siddhartha pleasure palaces and forbade anyone who was sick or old to come near the prince. He also ordered Siddhartha never to leave his palaces. Siddhartha grew up surrounded by beautiful things and people, shielded from the anguish and suffering of the real world.

At age sixteen, Siddhartha married a beautiful girl and they had a son. His life seemed to be exactly as his father had hoped. Siddhartha became bored with his life of luxury, however, and one day convinced his charioteer to take him riding outside the palace grounds. What he saw would change his life. He saw a sick man, a frail old man, and a funeral, with relatives weeping over the corpse. He also came across a monk, peaceful and contented. Disturbed by what he saw, his curiosity was aroused and Siddhartha decided to find out the truth about human suffering and existence.

Siddhartha's search for enlightenment

Siddhartha gave up his life of ease and even left his wife and son to search for the truth. He cut off his hair, put on the yellow robe of a wandering monk, and begged for his food. He spent the next six years learning from great teachers and lived for a while with ascetic (pronounced uh-SEH-tik) monks. Ascetic monks practice extreme self-denial. For example, they may go for long periods without food or sleep. After almost starving to death, Siddhartha realized that deliberately ill-treating the body was not the way to truth.

Siddhartha had now followed two extremes in his life, one of luxury and pleasure and one of asceticism. Both left him still hungry for the truth, so he decided to embark on "the Middle Path," a way of life between these two extremes. Along this path, he would eventually achieve insight and wisdom, which would lead to peace and enlightenment.

"To satisfy the necessities of life is not evil," he concluded. "To keep the body in good health is a duty, for otherwise we shall not be able to trim the lamp of wisdom, and keep our mind strong and clear." The Middle Path would become a major belief of Buddhism, advocating balance between extremes and avoiding any particular things or ideas produced by selfish desires. The best way to travel the Middle Path is through meditation, following in the Buddha's footsteps.

Siddhartha's awakening

Siddhartha resolved to meditate until he discovered the truth about life and suffering and how to become free of pain. He came upon a great tree, called the bodhi tree (pronounced BOH-dee; tree of wisdom), and sat beneath it to meditate. At long last, at the age of thirty-five, he achieved a state of enlightenment, or knowledge of the true nature of being and suffering. He entered a state of perfect peace and joy, *nirvana.*

Having achieved enlightenment, he became the Buddha or "the Enlightened One" and understood "the Four Noble Truths," which became the core of his teaching: (1) Suffering is universal; (2) The cause of suffering is the attempt to satisfy selfish cravings or desires; (3) Suffering can be stopped by overcoming selfish desires; (4) The way to end craving and suffering is to follow the Eightfold Path, eight steps concerning the right way to think and conduct oneself.

Meditation

An important part of Buddhism is meditation, a practice that Buddha is shown doing in most of his statues. Buddhists meditate to come to a better understanding of the Buddha's teachings (*dharma*). Many non-Buddhists use meditation to relieve stress and to achieve a sense of calm.

To meditate, a person sits on the floor, usually cross-legged, with the back and head erect. Buddha's spine was supposedly so rigid he could not turn his head to either side. Then the person lowers the eyelids, closing the eyes about halfway. Often the person focuses on his or her breath or chants to help in meditating. A person meditating tries to relax his mind and "go beneath it," sort of like diving under the waves of a rough lake and sitting on the bottom, where it is calm and peaceful.

In his first sermon, he told his listeners:

There are two extremes ... which you must always avoid. The life of pleasure is base, ignoble, contrary to the spirit, unworthy and vain. And the life of mortification is sad and unworthy and vain. From these two extremes ... the Perfect One has kept away, and he has discovered the way which passes through the middle and which leads to peace, to knowledge, to Enlightenment, to Nirvana.... This ... is the sacred truth about pain: birth, old age, sickness, death and separation from what is loved are pain. This is the origin of

The Noble Eightfold Path

1. Right seeing or understanding
2. Right thought
3. Right speech
4. Right action
5. Right livelihood
6. Right effort
7. Right mindfulness
8. Right contemplation

pain: it is the thirst for pleasure, the thirst for existence, the thirst for what is impermanent. And this is the truth about the suppression of pain: it is the quenching of the thirst by the abolition of desire.

Buddhists believe that those who do their best to follow the Eightfold Path throughout their successive lives will achieve enlightenment. According to Buddhism, people experience a continual cycle of birth, illness, death, and rebirth, called *samsara*. In the West, this cycle is known as "reincarnation." When a person frees himself from cravings and desires for things of this world, he is then freed from the cycle of rebirths and reaches nirvana, the final goal of all human striving.

For the next forty-five years, until his death, Siddhartha wandered through India teaching what he had learned and winning converts. Some of his followers became monks or nuns and, like the Buddha, wandered from place to place spreading his teachings. They were allowed to take with them only eight items: a robe, a belt, a beggar's bowl, a staff, a razor, a needle, a toothpick, and a strainer. The strainer was for removing any insects that might fall into their food or drink so that the insects would not be eaten. Buddha condemned taking the life of any living creature. Today, monks still are given some of these items, but they also receive other basics such as an umbrella and a warm coat.

During the rainy season, Buddha's followers would set up camp or resting places (*viharas*) to wait out the monsoon rains. These resting places marked the beginning of many of the great Buddhist monasteries that are scattered throughout Asia today.

Early Visakha Puja celebrations

According to early Buddhist texts, celebrations of Buddha Day date as far back as the first century before the birth of Jesus Christ, the founder of Christianity (c. 6 B.C.–c. A.D. 30). The primary activity in the early festivals was the bathing of Buddha images and parading Buddha statues on beautifully decorated floats or wagons. Washing the images was said to show respect for Buddha's ability to grant boons, or favors. By observing the procession of Buddha statues, one was thought to be pardoned of sinful deeds.

Visakha Puja is an ancient Thai (relating to Thailand) festival dating back to the fourteenth century, when Sukhothai (pronounced SOO-kuh-tie) was the capital of Thailand. The festival eventually died out, but in 1817 it was revived by Rama II (King Isara Southorn; 1768–1824).

Rama decreed a three-day holiday, one day for each of the three major events in Buddha's life: his birth, enlightenment, and death. The holiday was eventually reduced to a one-day event. Later in the nineteenth century, Rama IV (King Mongkut; 1804–1868) composed two prayers (*gathas*) in tribute to Buddha and his teachings that are still repeated on Buddha Day.

Folklore, Legends, Stories

As with other historical religious figures, it is difficult to separate the facts from legends surrounding Buddha's birth. Many of the legends and traditions associated with Buddha were passed down orally, beginning with Buddha's contemporaries. His teachings were not written down until about five hundred years after his death. Although many of the events surrounding Buddha's birth are shrouded in myth and legend, Buddhists believe they are factual.

The white elephant and the god Vishnu

According to one legend, Buddha was miraculously conceived. His mother, Queen Maya, dreamed one night that a white elephant (a good omen) with six tusks touched her side. At that instant, Buddha was conceived. King Shuddhodana summoned palace wise men to interpret the dream. According to the wise men, the dream meant that the child would grow up to be either a great king or a great ascetic, a holy man who would practice extreme self-denial and live in poverty, begging for his food.

One day as Maya was picking flowers in the palace garden, the child was born, emerging from her right side. He immediately stood up and took seven steps

A figure of a seated Buddha.
On Buddha Day, statues of the Buddha are bathed to wash away the dust and dirt of the year.

in each direction of the compass. Lotus flowers (also a good symbol) appeared in his footsteps. He then raised his right hand, lowered his left and announced, "Above heaven and below heaven, I alone am honored. No further births have I to endure, for this is my last body." Then a gentle rain fell on the baby.

Another legend about his birth holds that Buddha came from the navel of the Hindu god Vishnu. This is believed to symbolize that Buddhism has Hindu roots. Hinduism (pronounced HIN-doo-IZ-uhm) is the major religion of India and is built upon the belief of rebirth known as reincarnation. Buddha, himself, was a Hindu before his enlightenment.

"The Birthday of Buddha"

With my elder brother and younger sister
I, the youngest son, Chiaki, aged eleven,
accompany father, mother, elder sister
to the small temple at the end of our
    street.

At the other end of our street hangs like
    an old
wood-block print, beyond the grey tiled
    roofs
of little shops and houses, our divine
    Mount Fuji—
a lucky omen for this holy day—for Fuji-
    san
too often hides himself in smog or
    clouds.
But today the lingering last snows on his
    sacred peak
are sparkling in the pure blue heavens.

We are all wearing our best clothes—
my mother and sisters in bright spring
    kimono and zori,
we three men in good suits, shirts, ties,
    shoes.
But my father's carrying a folding paper
    fan.

At the temple gate, the smiling priest
bows his welcome, and we all bow
    deeply in return.
He sometimes plays baseball with us, but
    today
he is wearing formal robes.

We bow to the statue of the infant Bud-
    dha

standing inside his miniature temple
of spring greenery and pale-rose cherry-
    blossom.
He is shining in the happy sun. One by
    one,
we slowly pour over him ladles of sweet
    brown tea.
He always seems to enjoy it. He, too, is
    smiling.

The priest and his wife and children
    invite us
to take tea, the same festive tea we gave
    the Buddha,
with sweet cakes, satsumas and candies.

With folded hands, we bow farewell to
    Buddha,
and to the smiling priest, who bows
    farewell to us.

—But once outside the temple gate
my older brother and I dash home to
    change our clothes
for baseball practice in the field behind
    the temple,
where the infant Buddha goes on smiling
as if he, too, is on our team.

And at the end of our street, old Fuji-san
hangs like a crimson half-moon in the
    afterglow.

—James Kirkup

Source: Let's Celebrate, *compiled by John Foster. Oxford:
Oxford University Press, 1989, pp. 38–39.*

A Buddhist monk at a ceremony in Taipei, Taiwan, in 1998, holding a miniature pagoda containing a tooth believed to have belonged to Buddha. Buddhists say the tooth brings blessings for those who live where it is housed and shields them from disaster. Reproduced by permission of AP/Wide World Photos.

Buddhism's roots

In Sri Lanka, the oldest continually Buddhist country in the world, Buddhists pay reverence to a branch of the bodhi tree under which Buddha achieved enlightenment. According to legend, Indian king Asoka's daughter, a nun, planted the branch when she traveled there to teach Buddhism. The branch took root, as did the new religion.

The Jataka Tales

The Buddha is the reputed author of more than five hundred stories or fables known as the Jataka (pronounced juh-TAH-kuh) Tales, which are among the most famous folktales in the world. The tales are about the Buddha's previous lives and cover such issues as responsibility, friendship, honesty, ecology, and respect for elders.

They are more than two thousand years old but were not written down until several hundred years after Buddha's death. Before that time, they were memorized and passed down from generation to generation. Some of the scenes were carved into ancient monuments in India and can still be seen today. The Jatakas remain popular

Borobudur Temple, a ninth-century Buddhist monument in central Java.
Borobudur contains fifteen hundred panels illustrating Buddha's teachings and
four hundred statues of Buddha. Reproduced by permission of Susan D. Rock.

and have inspired drama and art in Asia through the centuries.

Included among the stories is a tree that asked to be cut down piece by piece in order to avoid hurting other plants, a hare that cooked himself to feed a starving beggar, and a vegetarian quail doomed to stay small because of his no-worm diet. One of these classic tales, about the elephant and the blind men, is one of the best-known parables in the world.

The elephant and the blind men: Several blind men lived in the same Indian village. In the forest one day, they came upon an elephant. Each of them described the part of the elephant he felt. One felt one of the elephant's tusks, another its tail, another its leg, and one felt its ear. The one who felt the tusk said it was a plow; the one who felt the tail, a rope; the one who felt the leg, a tree; and the one who felt the ear said the elephant was a fan. They began arguing about who was right and finally started hitting one another.

All four men were correct because they described the part of the elephant they felt. They could not feel the whole elephant, however, and so they could not describe or understand the whole animal. Likewise, the whole truth about schools of belief or religion is something that is beyond understanding, and often causes conflict and fighting.

Customs, Traditions, Ceremonies

Visakha Puja is a public holiday in many southeast Asian countries, including Thailand. It is one of the happiest days of the Buddhist year. People clean and decorate their houses for the celebration. Sacred books are dusted off and aired out. People visit temples at Buddhist monasteries to hear monks preach about the life of Buddha and to make offerings and receive blessings. The temples are beautifully decorated with flowers in many designs.

Statues of the Buddha, many covered with gold leaf (thin sheets of gold), are taken from their resting places and washed with scented water, or with hydrangea tea in Japan. This practice symbolizes purification and faith in goodness and peace on earth. After an image of Buddha is bathed, it is dressed in a new robe contributed by a worshiper. People also water bodhi trees at monasteries in remembrance of Buddha's achieving enlightenment under such a tree.

On the evening of Visakha Puja, statues of the Buddha in temples are decorated with lights and candles to celebrate Buddha's enlightenment. Monks and crowds of worshipers holding candles or lamps, decorated with flowers in many beautiful designs, walk around the statues in a clockwise circle. This practice, called *wien tien* (circling with the candle) in Thailand, began as a ritual to secure a peaceful death and safe passage to nirvana, the Buddhist paradise. It gradually became a folk custom, and today people sing songs and pray as they circle. Later in the evening, as the candles slowly burn out and darkness descends, monks chant a sermon prepared especially for the service.

Peace and goodwill

The true spirit of Buddhism is said to shine through on Visakha Puja. One of Buddha's main teachings involves the concept of *metta,* or "loving kindness." He preached that through metta one can overcome anger through love, evil through good, and untruth through truth. He also said, "Always think compassion. That is all you need to know." On his birthday, Buddhists in Thailand and around the world wish people everywhere peace and abundance in the spirit of metta.

Celebrations

The major celebrations on Buddha Day for Buddhists in Thailand center on events at the temple. There they chant passages from Buddhist teachings and carry offerings of incense, flowers, and candles to show their love and respect for Buddha.

Buddha Day is a time of rejoicing in Sri Lanka. People decorate their houses and place offerings of flowers and fresh fruits before statues of the Buddha. After the ceremonies, the fruit is eaten by Buddhist priests. Homes and temples are also adorned with lights and paper lanterns, lighting up the night and filling the air with the sweet smell of coconut oil. Loudspeakers play music and stories about the Buddha's life. Huge paintings depicting the life of Buddha are displayed.

In the evenings, the celebrants sit outside in the moonlight and listen to long sermons by the priests. The "sermons" are actually readings, however, and are usually taken from the Jataka Tales. People sometimes sit outside all night, dressed in their best clothes, and listen to the tales and chat with their neighbors between readings.

In many countries, such as Japan, there are lantern processions in the streets. These parades are an important part of the celebration, and people look forward to seeing thousands of lights flickering in the dark. The lights symbolize hope, and the festival is sometimes called the Feast of the Lanterns.

In Japan, the festival is also known as Hana Matsuri (pronounced HAH-nuh mot-SIR-ee), or the Flower Festival, because the cherry trees are in blossom. People who visit temples and shrines are expected to carry offerings of cherry blossoms. Japanese Buddhist women wear their nicest kimonos (pronounced kuh-MOH-nohs), long robes with wide sleeves, worn with a wide sash or belt, on Hana Matsuri.

In South Korea, families go to Buddhist temples to worship. People decorate their homes and display paper lanterns. They used to build towers to hang the lanterns from, one for each member of the family. It was believed that the brighter the lanterns burned, the luckier the family would be. As in Japan, the lanterns were in the shape of carp (a fish), turtles, and other animal designs as well as flowers.

In ancient times, the eight gates of Seoul (the capital of South Korea), which were locked at nightfall, were left open and people could roam around and visit until midnight. Today's celebrations are like neighborhood block parties, with traditional instrumental music blaring from trucks, children beating drums, and lots of food. Firecrackers are also part of the fun.

A major celebration takes place in central Java at the Mendut Temple, a ninth-century Buddhist monument. Buddhists from Sri Lanka and other countries attend. Celebrants walk one and a half miles from the Mendut Temple to the Borobudur Temple, also built in the ninth century. Borobudur contains fifteen hundred panels illustrating Buddha's teachings and four hundred statues of Buddha.

When they reach the huge statue of Buddha located at the top of the temple, the people circle it in a clockwise direction. The men wear saffron (orange-colored) robes and the women wear white sārīs (pronounced SAH-reez), a garment consisting of a long length of cloth first wrapped about the waist and then draped over the shoulder. They all walk barefoot and carry candles. When they finish, they recite prayers, listen to sermons by the monks, and meditate.

A big blast

In Thailand and Laos, a big festival held in conjunction with Buddha Day is the Boun Bang Fai, or Rocket Festival. The festival, held on the first full moon of May, originated as a rain ceremony, invoking the gods to provide a lot of rain to ensure a good rice harvest. Today, it is one of the wildest celebrations in Laos with music and dancing, processions, and merrymaking. The celebration ends with the firing of bamboo rockets into the sky, a way of asking the heavens to begin the rainy season and bring water to the rice fields. Prizes go to individuals who launch the fastest, highest, and brightest rockets.

In Thailand, the celebration is usually held on the second weekend in May and is especially festive in the eastern city of Yasothon. The two-day festival begins with parades, beauty pageants, dances, par-

A square in Phoenix, Arizona, decorated with Japanese carp windsocks. Today's celebrations are like neighborhood block parties, with traditional instrumental music blaring from trucks, kids beating drums, and lots of food. Reproduced by permission of Phoenix Parks, Recreation and Library Department.

ties, dressing in disguise, and entertainment—much like Carnival in the West. As in other Asian countries, the main attraction is shooting off huge rockets. In the past, the competition to see whose rocket would stay aloft the longest generated free-for-all mud fights between rival teams.

The rockets are made of long bamboo poles fitted with short pieces of polyvinyl chloride (PVC) pipe containing gunpowder and water. They are beautifully decorated with dragons and other creatures and with colored streamers. The rockets are launched from a wooden scaffold. In earlier times, they were lit by hand, often with disastrous consequences. Today, they are launched by remote electrical ignition, although celebrations are not without a few injuries or deaths when the homemade missiles go astray.

In 1999, four people were killed and eleven others injured in Yasothon. The four were killed when an almost 500-pound rocket plummeted to the ground and exploded after rising about 100 feet into the air.

Although the Rocket Festival was originally a religious holiday, today it is celebrated by people from many faiths. The Rocket Festival has been celebrated by Southeast Asian immigrants to the United States since the 1970s. Rather than securing rain and a good rice harvest, in the United States the festival celebrates Asian ethnicity (religious and cultural background).

Clothing, Costumes

Many Thai Buddhists dress in their best clothes on Buddha Day to attend the ceremonies at temples. Others, to show their mourning for the passing away of Buddha, do not wear jewelry or perfume and dress very simply. In Sri Lanka, many older people dress in white and spend the holiday meditating in temples.

Foods, Recipes

Buddhists enjoy a ceremonial food called *hta-ma-ne* (sticky rice with coconut) at Buddha Day celebrations. It is cooked in a large pot on the grounds of a monastery and given as an offering to monks and the general public. Large hardwood paddles are used to stir the thick, sticky mixture.

Making merit

In the morning on Buddha Day, devout Buddhists who wish to "make merit" with Buddha, meaning they are trying to get credits toward a "good" rebirth, carry food to the temples for the monks. Many people set up stands and offer free food and drinks to passersby, in remembrance of Buddha's call to be kind to others.

Tea time

In Japan, Buddhists ladle sweet tea on the image of Buddha on his birthday because, according to legend, it rained tea on the day he was born. Afterward, they drink tea as a symbolic cleansing and display of their wish to become like Buddha.

Symbols

Symbols associated with Buddhism and the celebration of Buddha's birthday include the dharma wheel, the lotus flower, and the various images of Buddha.

The dharma wheel

The primary symbol of Buddhism is a wheel with eight spokes, called the dharma wheel. Dharma refers to the teachings of Buddha, which Buddhists believe were not invented by Buddha but are laws of nature that have always existed. The eight spokes are a reminder of the eight ways of living and thinking, or the Eightfold Path to Enlightenment, taught by Buddha. Because dharma refers to Buddha's teaching, his first sermon, which was given at modern-day Sarnath in northern India, is referred to as "the first turning of the wheel of dharma."

The dharma wheel also symbolizes samsara, the belief that life consists of constant cycles of change, of beginnings and endings, of birth, death, and rebirth—like a wheel that is always spinning.

Lotus

Buddhists collect lotus flowers, a type of water lily, to display during Visakha Puja. The lotus is a Buddhist symbol of purity and goodness and the enlightened mind. It starts life in the mud at the bottom of a wet area and rises to the top, unsoiled by the mud it grows in. This is symbolic of how people can rise above bad or unpleasant things to achieve enlightenment. One legend about Buddha's birth holds that he was born from a lotus plant and that lotus blossoms appeared in his first seven footsteps.

The Buddha image

On Buddha Day, many Buddhists carry baskets containing offerings of flowers and choice fruits to temples and place them before statues of the Buddha. In a symbolic purification, statues of the Buddha are taken outside the temple and bathed or sprinkled with water to wash away the dust and dirt of the year. New robes are then placed on the statues. The practice is said to stem from an event at Buddha's birth when two snakes bathed him after he was born. According to another story, nine dragons appeared from heaven and baptized Buddha at birth.

The thousands of different images of the Buddha include any number of symbolic meanings. For instance, the teaching Buddha is usually depicted sitting with one hand raised. When his right hand is touching the ground, he is calling on Earth to witness his teachings. When he is lying down, he is at the end of his life, just before entering nirvana.

There are also many symbols indicating that Buddha was not an ordinary man. For example, he is frequently depicted with a bump on his head, indicating that he had special gifts. He often has a round mark resembling a third eye on his forehead, a sign that he could see things most people cannot. Another frequently occurring symbol is the halo-like "nimbus of glory," which takes various forms and illustrates the Buddha's enlightenment. His

Hta-Ma-Ne

Ingredients

4 cups cooked glutinous rice, kept warm (available at Asian food stores)

⅓ cup peanut butter

1½ tablespoons finely grated fresh ginger or 1 teaspoon ground ginger

1 tablespoon vegetable oil

3 tablespoons fresh garlic, finely chopped

3 tablespoons toasted sesame seeds

½ cup shredded coconut

Directions

1. Heat oil in a medium saucepan and stir together cooked rice, peanut butter, ginger, garlic, sesame seeds, and coconut.
2. Cover and cook over low heat for about 10 minutes to heat through, stirring occasionally.

Serves 4

long ear lobes indicate that he came from an aristocratic family. And his hair is usually curled, symbolizing that he was a very holy man.

Music, Dance

On Visakha Puja, there are plays and dances to celebrate the holiday. For the dances, Thais wear headdresses and brightly colored outfits in traditional colors of red, green, white, and gold.

For More Information

Bancroft, Anne. *The Buddhist World*. Morristown, N.J.: Silver Burdett, 1985.

Penney, Sue. *Buddhism*. Austin, Tex.: Raintree Steck-Vaughn, 1997.

Rawding, F. W. *The Buddha*. Minneapolis, Minn.: Lerner Publications, n.d.

Winchester, Faith. *Asian Holidays*. Mankato, Minn.: Capstone Press, 1996.

Web sites

"Buddha.net: Buddhist Information Network." [Online] http://www.buddhanet.net (accessed on January 23, 2000).

Buddha's Birthday Sources

Angell, Carole S. *Celebrations Around the World*. Golden, Colo.: Fulcrum Publishing, 1996, pp. 47, 74.

"Buddhism." In *The Illustrated Encyclopedia of World Religions,* edited by Chris Richards. Rockport, Mass.: Element Books, 1997, pp. 86–111.

Fontein, Jan. "Notes on the Jatakas and Avadanas of Barabudur." In *Barabadur: History and Significance of a Buddhist Monument,* edited by Luis Gomez and Hiram W. Woodward Jr. Berkeley, Calif.: Institute of Buddhist Studies, 1981, pp. 85–108.

Gerson, R. *Traditional Festivals in Thailand*. Oxford: Oxford University Press, 1996, p. 6.

Ho, Siow Yen. *South Korea*. Milwaukee, Wis.: Gareth Stevens, 1998, pp. 12–15.

Peck, Grant. "Thailand's Rocket Festival." *Houston Chronicle,* June 27, 1999, p. 9G.

Santino, Jack. *All Around the Year: Holidays and Celebrations in American Life*. Chicago: University of Illinois Press, 1994.

Scanlon, Phil Jr. *Southeast Asia: A Cultural Study Through Celebration*. DeKalb, Ill.: Center for Southeast Asian Studies, Northern Illinois University, 1985, p. 75.

Snelling, John. *Buddhist Festivals*. Vero Beach, Fla.: Rourke Enterprises, 1987, pp. 18, 23.

Wangu, Madhu Bazaz. *Buddhism*. New York: Facts On File, 1993.

Webb, Lois Sinaiko. *Holidays of the World Cookbook for Students*. Phoenix, Ariz.: Oryx Press, 1995, p. 167.

Web sites

"Buddhism: The Way of Wisdom." [Online] http://www.uucava.org/buddha.htm (accessed on January 15, 2000).

Mahinda, Bikkhu. "The Significance of Vesak." [Online] http://www.saigon.com/~anson/ebud/ebdha026.htm (accessed on January 23, 2000).

Carnival

Also Known As:
Carnaval (Brazil)
Karneval (Germany)
Fastnacht, Fasching, or Fasnet (Germany)
Carnevale (Italy)
Carnival (Trinidad and Tobago, United States)
Mardi Gras (United States)

Introduction

In the Christian religion, Lent is a forty-day period of spiritual preparation for one of the most joyous Christian festivals, Easter. Lent has traditionally been a time for asking forgiveness, fasting (abstaining from food or certain kinds of food, like meat), and spiritual self-examination. Over time, the practice of fasting has been replaced by the sacrifice or giving up of special treats or pastimes, such as desserts or watching television.

Before Lent, however, comes Carnival, a time of revelry and celebration. In most countries, the biggest celebrations are held on the Sunday, Monday (Shrove Monday), and Tuesday (Shrove Tuesday) just before Lent begins on Ash Wednesday. Shrove Tuesday, appropriately called Fat Tuesday, is a day for eating food that must be used up before Lent begins. It is also a time for parties and parades, costumes and masquerades, drinking and singing.

History

Most historians agree that Carnival, in its present form, began between about A.D. 1000 and 1300 as a way to ease the transition from the season of Epiphany to the sacrifices of Lent. According to Christian tradition, Epiphany commemorates the visit of the Three Wise Men or Three Kings who first recognized and worshiped the infant Jesus. During Lent, the Catholic Church did not allow people to eat meat or to marry, and it discouraged sexual relations.

The word "carnival" is said to come from the Latin *carnem levare,* which means "to take meat [or flesh] away." According to scholars, this definition could have a double meaning: to give up eating meat and, also, to do without other pleasures.

Writings dating to 1140 in Rome say that people paraded through the city and then slaughtered cattle for a feast before Lent. By the fourteenth century, carnivals in Rome and a number of other European cities were becoming yearly events. During the fifteenth and sixteenth centuries, the celebrations grew. Carnival became very popular among kings and queens in France, Italy, and Spain, and many of the symbols and activities still carried out today were created during this

Holiday Fact Box: Carnival

Themes

Feasting; drinking; parades; masquerades and balls; music and dancing; beauty contests; poking fun at political and public figures and current events.

Type of Holiday

Carnival is a secular (nonreligious) folk festival that occurs immediately before Lent, the six-week period of fasting that precedes Easter, which is one of the most sacred times of the year for Christians.

When Celebrated

Carnival, like Easter, is a movable holiday, but it usually falls during February. Carnival comes during pre-Lent, the time between Epiphany (January 6) and Ash Wednesday, which is the first day of Lent. Mardi Gras, also known as Shrove Tuesday or Fat Tuesday, is the final day of Carnival, and the one on which the biggest celebrations are held. Mardi Gras is always celebrated forty-six days before Easter.

time. Toward the end of the Middle Ages, people added elements of ancient Greek, Roman, and Egyptian festivals.

Carnival featured private masked balls and operas for the wealthy, but it also included public masked balls and cheap food and drink for the cities' crowds of common people. Street parades featured loud bands of musicians walking or riding on wagons and carts, and people shouting insults at one another and making fun of the wealthy ruling class and current events.

In early England, Shrove Tuesday was a day when Christians asked God for forgiveness from their sins. They also feasted on pancakes as they used up eggs, lard, and butter in preparation for Lenten fasting. As a consequence, Shrove Tuesday became known as Pancake Tuesday.

The Monday before Shrove Tuesday was called Collop Monday; the word "collop" means a slice of meat. This was the day to use up any fresh meat that would spoil during Lent. In France, it was customary to lead a fattened ox or cow through the streets as a reminder to give up eating red meat during Lent.

During the 1600s and 1700s, as the Catholic Church undertook reform and put in place stricter rules, churches in Europe tried to stop the wild parading and misbehavior that was part of Carnival. The Church's attempts at banning Carnival failed because people enjoyed the festival so much they did not want to stop the tradition.

In 1748, Pope Benedict XIV started a church ritual called "The Forty Hours of Carnival." Catholic churches were to be kept open for the three days before Lent so people could pray for forgiveness for their un-Christian behavior during Carnival. Special masses were held during the evenings. This custom remains today in many Catholic churches in cities where Carnival is held.

It was the French who introduced Carnival customs to the Americas during

Thousands enjoy the festivities in the streets of Orangestad, Aruba, during the 1998 Carnival celebrations. Lent has traditionally been a time for asking forgiveness, fasting, and spiritual self-examination. Before Lent, however, comes Carnival. Reproduced by permission of AP/Wide World Photos.

the 1700s when French colonizers settled in New Orleans, Louisiana, and Mobile, Alabama, and took control in parts of South America and the Caribbean. The Spanish and Portuguese also carried their Carnival customs to South and Central America. Rio de Janeiro (pronounced ree-oh day zhuh-NAIR-oh), Brazil, holds what is believed to be the largest Carnival celebration in the world.

In the Americas, European Carnival customs blended with the rituals of the native people and those of the African peo-ple who were brought to work the planta-tions as slaves. This creative mix of cultures helped make Carnival the extravagant festival that it is today.

Folklore, Legends, Stories

The themes chosen for Carnival parade floats, masquerade bands, and costume balls often reflect the history, mythology, and folklore of a culture. Social and political issues, in particular, are addressed in songs and speeches, in parade themes, in plays, and in costumes, making Carnival a

Tzeltal Maya Indians celebrate Carnival in Polocum, Mexico, in 1998. Thousands gathered in this Chiapas highlands village to celebrate Carnival with a mix of Catholic and Maya traditions. Reproduced by permission of AP/Wide World Photos.

reliable record of public feeling about leaders and events. In time, this record becomes part of a culture's folklore.

For example, one group of Brazilian Carnival dancers acts out the sacred music and ceremonies of the ancient African religion known as *candomblé*. Another reenacts the capture of East Africans who were shipped to Brazil as slaves to work on plantations. A native Indian folklore group dresses in native costume and performs a dance that tells the story of how Europeans overtook Indian villages as they colonized Brazil.

In Germany, folklore about the "child eater" and the "fool gobbler," as well as the "wild man" and the "fool" have been carried over into contemporary Carnival celebrations. Italians love to tell stories about the Miller's Daughter, who saved her people from a cruel landowner and now plays an important role in Carnival parades and festivities in Ivrea, Italy.

Caribbean folklore characters such as Callaloo and the Mancrab, the king of the forest, the she-devil, and mischievous little creatures called Douens can all be found in Carnival parades and costume contests. In the United States, "mystick" societies in New Orleans, Mobile, Alabama, and other cities rely on early Greek and Roman mythology as well as seventeenth-century English literature for their Carnival inspiration.

Customs, Traditions, Ceremonies

Every country—and every city—that celebrates Carnival has its unique customs and activities, many of them dating back hundreds of years. Large parades are common to every Carnival celebration, as are masquerading, feasting, and drinking. In large cities, formal and informal balls are so popular and so elaborate that people form secret clubs, known as "krewes" in New Orleans, to specifically plan Carnival events.

People also love Carnival for its music and dancing and for the familiar costumed figures that reappear each year. Tourists descend by the thousands on cities such as Rio de Janeiro, Port-of-Spain on the island of Trinidad, and New Orleans to be part of the world-famous Carnival events.

Symbolic opening and closing ceremonies accompany Carnival celebrations everywhere. Opening ceremonies include the eating of king's cakes in New Orleans on Epiphany. King's cakes are round or oval cakes striped with frosting in purple, gold, and green, the symbolic colors of Carnival, which represent justice, power, and faith. A tiny figure is hidden inside the cakes; the person who finds the figure in his or her cake must buy the next cake or host the next king's ball. Another opening ceremony is the pre-dawn J'ouvert (pronounced zhoo-VAIR; opening day) parade in Trinidad.

Closing ceremonies sometimes involve burning, burying, or otherwise disposing of a figure representing Carnival and its excesses. After several days of parties, people faithfully attend Lenten church services on Ash Wednesday, even if they have been up all night on Fat Tuesday.

Crowning of royalty

The crowning of a king and a queen is common to most Carnival celebrations. The royal couple rides on a richly decorated float in Carnival parades and is usually attended by a Carnival court of noble men and women. To commemorate Shrove Tuesday (the day before Lent begins), the couple is usually given the keys to the city for a day.

The custom of crowning a king and queen to reign over Carnival madness is believed to have started when wealthy European landowners allowed servants or slaves to establish make-believe or temporary kingdoms. The purpose of these temporary kingdoms was either to help citizens take care of conflicts within their own community or to allow them to have a little fun during the holiday.

The Carnival king and queen are usually chosen well ahead of Shrove Tuesday. In New Orleans, where keeping identities hidden is important to the organizations that plan Carnival, known as krewes, the Carnival king is the only member of the krewe to reveal his identity.

In Trinidad, King and Queen Carnival are chosen on the basis of their elaborate costumes. Trinidad also crowns kings from different musical groups; the best singers lead parades as "monarchs." Even children are included in the Carnival royal-

A person dressed as Ziripot, representing the strongest man of the village, parades through the streets of Lanz, Spain, during Carnival in 1998. Reproduced by permission of AP/Wide World Photos.

is fierce for king and queen of Carnival, and winning the title depends on having the most stunning costume.

In Italy, France, Germany, and Belgium, traditional costumes that date to the 1500s and 1600s are still copied and worn every year. In Belgium, one of society's great honors for men is to march as one of the Gilles (pronounced ZHEEL), a specially picked group who dress alike and wear identical masks and great plumed headgear, in a Carnival parade. Large groups of people dressed in costumes on a particular theme, such as modern fairy tales or mythology, are the highlight of Carnival parades in Rio de Janeiro and in Port-of-Spain.

People who do not march in a parade but enjoy the sights and sounds as spectators also like to dress in costume. Brazilians have a perfect word for costumes, *fantasia* (pronounced fon-TAZH-ah), because Carnival is a time when everyone is encouraged to act out their fantasies, at least for a day. People dress as animals or as fictional, historical, current, or mythological characters. Another costume tradition that has developed over time is to switch identities: men often dress as women and women as men.

ty. A children's king and queen of Carnival ride on fancy floats just as the adults do.

Clothing, Costumes

Carnival is often referred to as "the greatest show on earth," and the show is all about costume. The more wild and colorful and outrageous a costume is, the better. Costume designers spend all year creating magnificent outfits that will bring cheers from the crowds that come for Carnival. The competition in Trinidad, for example,

Foods, Recipes

Because Carnival comes directly before a period of fasting and abstinence, food and feasting is an essential component of the holiday. Part of the Carnival tradition in many countries is eating pastries that are deep fried in fat, like doughnuts. This is because Shrove Tuesday has traditionally been the time to use up household stores of animal fat, eggs, butter, and meat, which people were forbidden to eat during Lent.

The Gilles of Binche

Belgium, a European country that lies between France and Germany, is famous for its Carnival celebrations held throughout the nation. The most well known takes places on Fat Tuesday in the town of Binche (pronounced BANSH). On this day, the prominent men of society dress in identical costumes and march in a parade. They are known as the Gilles (pronounced ZHEEL) of Binche.

Approximately nine hundred men belonging to about ten societies put on identical wax masks with thin mustaches, hats with tall plumes made of curled white ostrich feathers, and matching suits that are unusually patterned or striped and trimmed with braid. The headdresses can weigh up to seven pounds and stand four feet high. Each man's costume is stuffed with rolls of straw to make the chest look full and padded.

The Gilles march and dance through the streets to traditional drumbeats and to the jangling of the bells each Gille wears around his waist on a leather band. They also carry oranges in wicker baskets, which are thrown at the crowds gathered along the Grand-Rue, Main Street, to watch the parade. Everyone holds out his hand to catch the oranges; it is considered bad manners to throw them back. In years past, the Gilles threw apples, onions, and walnuts instead of oranges.

According to legend, the Gilles's dance was first performed in the early 1500s at a festival that Queen Mary of Hungary, the Lady of Binche, organized to honor King Philip II of Spain. The seven-day celebration included balls, simulations of military actions, banquets, and fireworks displays.

The event occurred during a period of Spanish exploration of the Americas. The Spanish explorers, just back from their travels, told tales of the Inca, South American Indians living in what is now Peru. They especially enjoyed describing the rituals performed by the Inca and the colorful costumes worn during them. According to some stories, several Inca brought from their native land to Binche attended the ceremony. The citizens of Binche are said to have been so impressed with the Incan costumes that they made it a tradition to dress up as Inca every year.

The dance the Gilles perform today is believed to have been part of an Inca ritual observed by the Spaniards. The Gilles have performed the dance each year for the past four hundred years, making it among the oldest of Carnival traditions.

In Great Britain, Shrove Tuesday became known as Pancake Tuesday, because families used up these ingredients by making feasts of pancakes. Fritters, doughnuts, and other pastries, deep-fried and coated with powdered sugar, are traditional Carnival foods in Germany, France, Italy, and New Orleans.

Traditional meat, bean, and vegetable dishes are often prepared in large quantities for Carnival feasts. In Italy, whole towns are invited to come out and share in these feasts. Such foods often have historical or folkloric significance. For example, in Brazil, people cook dishes made from various cuts of pork, because leftover pork was once given to African slaves in that country during Carnival.

Along with the bounty of food comes an abundance of alcoholic beverages. In many cities, Carnival is one big street party with free-flowing drinks, especially beer, all day and night. In southern climates, people also drink lots of fruity nonalcoholic beverages.

Arts, Crafts, Games

Carnival, probably more than any other holiday, offers an opportunity to put artistic talents to work. Whether a person designs and makes his or her own costume or relies on one of the many gifted costume designers and seamstresses, a tremendous amount of effort goes into creating a Carnival costume. Designing Carnival costumes has made more than one artist famous— Peter Minshall of Trinidad, for example, has gained fame by creating many prize-winning king and queen costumes.

Designing and building parade floats is another area where artists and craftspeople are in demand. The massive floats can take months to build. Costume and float design are true works of art and their creators true artists, with the streets and large arenas and auditoriums their galleries. These creative works are seen not only by those who attend Carnival celebra-tions but by millions of people who watch the televised versions worldwide.

Carnival games and "throws"

Since the early days of Carnival, people have amused themselves and their fellow citizens with a number of Carnival games and pretend fights. Italy had some of the most interesting diversions. One tradition involved sliding a paper dove down a rope from the town bell tower. As the dove progressed down the rope, it spilled confetti on the crowds. Bullfights were held in the narrow streets of Venice, and the famous Carnival orange fights are still held in the town of Ivrea.

Throwing favors, such as cheap plastic bead necklaces and imitation doubloons (old gold coins of Spain and Spanish America), from parade floats into the crowd is a major part of Mardi Gras in New Orleans. In Germany, people are pelted with flowers, candy, and other throws. In Binche (pronounced BANSH), Belgium, the otherwise-dignified Gilles throw oranges at the crowd. In times past, throughout Europe and the Americas, such strange things as flour, eggs, dirt, plaster-coated seeds, and onions have been hurled at festival-goers.

Symbols

An integral symbol of Carnival is King Carnival, who is often represented as a fat man, because overeating and drinking too much are characteristic of the pre-Lenten holiday. In many European countries, King Carnival has long been a symbolic figure that is revered during the crazy days of Carnival and then done away with just before the beginning of Lent. As a scapegoat for the sins and excesses of the

Haitians dressed in Chinese tiger costumes parade through the streets of Jacmel during Carnival in 1998. Carnival, probably more than any other holiday, offers an opportunity to put artistic talents to work. Reproduced by permission of AP/Wide World Photos.

people during Carnival, the king—often represented as a straw man—is dragged out of town and buried, burned, drowned, shot, or hanged to get rid of the "evil" he has represented.

The fool or clown

In ancient times, a person who was considered mentally unfit was known as a "fool." Because they were mentally challenged, fools had the freedom to say and do whatever they pleased. Eventually, persons "playing the fool" were often kept by kings and queens for entertainment because they could make up funny, clever, or witty rhymes, songs, or plays about people and events.

The fool has always played an important part in Carnival celebrations, although he is represented in many different ways depending upon the country and the culture. The fool is at the center of Carnival parades, and he is allowed to make speeches criticizing and ridiculing government officials, famous people, and political issues. In Trinidad, this type of social comment is heard in calypso (pronounced kuh-LIP-soh) songs.

The fool dressed as a clown is a traditional folklore character that appears in the Carnival costumes of many countries. He was made famous in the Italian theater *commedia dell'arte* (pronounced kom-AID-ee-uh del-AR-tay) as Pierrot (pronounced pyair-ROH), the sad-faced clown in the oversized coat.

The French adapted Pierrot for their own Carnival, and French planters took the character to the Caribbean, where he later became Pierrot Grenade (pronounced pyair-ROW greh-NOD), a ferocious clownlike figure who fought with whips and sticks. The multicolored clown Harlequin; the clown in the checkered overalls, Burlamacco; and the raggedy, patchwork court jester Farinella also originated in Italy.

Early "fools" in Germany were central to rituals that celebrated the coming of spring. Young men would dress in rags, grow their hair and beards long, and run about the countryside acting like wild men. Fools may have evolved as a way to laugh at the world after the horrors of the bubonic plague, an epidemic of a highly contagious and deadly disease, also known as the Black Death, which wiped out much of the population of Europe in the 1300s. Eventually, fools' societies became responsible for planning Carnival events in Germany, and have continued to do so to the present.

Today, Carnival is a time to "act the fool," or behave in ways a person normally would not. It is a time to dress in wild costumes, to make fun of the world, and to turn life upside down for a short time. For this reason, Carnival is referred to as "the crazy days," and the fool is one of its major symbols.

Fried pastries or pancakes

Shrove Tuesday, or the day just before Ash Wednesday, occurred during a time of year when households were running out of fresh meats, eggs, butter, and animal fat at the end of winter. Because these foods were nearly used up and people would soon have to do without them for a time anyway, the Church designated the six weeks before Easter as Lent, a time to fast and to repent from sin. Knowing that Lent was soon coming, families hurried to use up what little was left of these forbidden foods.

A good use for them was to mix the eggs and butter with flour and fry them in the animal fat, making either pancakes or a type of fried pastry. Coating the pastries with sugar made them especially tasty so they would be eaten up quickly. Each culture adapted the recipe, and eating fried pastries or pancakes on Shrove Tuesday, and throughout the Carnival season, became a tradition that has lasted for hundreds of years.

In Great Britain, Shrove Tuesday is famous for pancakes. Some towns hold pancake races, in which housewives compete in a footrace while flipping pancakes in a skillet. In Germany, and in communities with German heritage in the United States, people love to eat *fastnachtkuchen* (pronounced FAHS-nockt-coo-ken), big round doughnuts that are sometimes filled with jelly. Italian towns each have their own special light, ribbonlike pastry, called by a number of odd names, like "little lies," "gossips," and "nuns' ribbons."

In France and French-influenced New Orleans, it is the square fritter without a hole called the *beignet* (pronounced ben-YAY) that is popular. Pastries are not eaten as often in Brazil, but a Carnival dinner

A fire thrower pleases the crowds of thousands gathered in the streets of Panama City, Panama, to celebrate Carnival in 1999. Reproduced by permission of AP/Wide World Photos.

might include a fried flour dish made from a starchy tropical root called manioc (pronounced MAN-ee-ahk).

Music, Dance

Wherever there are Carnival celebrations, there is music and dance, and Carnival—especially in Trinidad and Tobago and in Brazil—is an occasion for music and dancing like no other time of year. Carnival has made calypso and the steel drum music of Trinidad and Tobago world famous.

In New Orleans, jazz and rhythm and blues performers spice up Carnival; in Italy, it is the classical music of the great composers. In Germany, calypso takes on a different form with music and dance groups called *buettenredner* (pronounced BUE-ten-red-ner), which mock prominent people and everyday life. Folk music is also very popular.

Among the most well-known pieces of Carnival music are "If Ever I Cease to Love," "Iko Iko," and "Go to the Mardi Gras," made famous in New Orleans; *Carnival in Venice,* a classical piece from Italy; and "Jean and Dinah," a calypso classic by the group Mighty Sparrow from Trinidad.

When crowds gather to celebrate Carnival, they not only want to hear loud music, but they want to dance. In Trinidad, people do a dance called "jump up" to the steel drum and calypso bands. Brazil is famous for giving birth to the African-based dance called the samba.

Brazil

Name of Holiday: Carnaval

Introduction

Brazil is the largest of the South American countries, and its Carnaval (pronounced car-na-VAHL) in the coastal city of Rio de Janeiro (pronounced ree-oh day zhuh-NAIR-oh) is said to be the largest and wildest in the world. Other Brazilian coastal cities, including Salvador (in the state of Bahia), Recife (pronounced ri-SEE-fee), Belem, and São Paulo, also celebrate Carnaval.

Preparation for Carnaval goes on all year in Rio, and city businesses and offices close during the week or two before the celebration. Everyone gets a holiday from work to dress in costumes and join in the parades. The actual festival lasts from the Saturday through Tuesday before Ash Wednesday. February is one of the hottest months in Brazil, which lies south of the equator, so Carnaval is a steamy, summertime celebration.

History

The Portuguese carried the European celebration of Carnival with them when they settled in Brazil during the 1500s. In the early years, the Portuguese wore masks and sprayed one another with flour and water during Carnival parades to create bizarre-looking white faces and bodies. This practice has been carried over into the Brazilian custom of tossing colored flour water or confetti into the faces of people in the streets during Carnaval.

Masquerade balls were introduced in Rio in 1846 by a French actress who was living in the city. The African slaves who worked on the plantations were not allowed to take part in the fancy balls held by the Portuguese landowners, but they were given a day off to hold their own private celebrations, with African drumming and dancing in the streets. They wore whatever costumes they could put together and sometimes whitewashed themselves to imitate the free whites.

In 1907, a group of black, white, and mixed-blood artisans and craftspeople formed a "promenade" group for Carnaval, with singing, drumming, and flute playing; the ladies dressed in European fashions. They called themselves "Delightful Myrtle" and chose specific themes for their theatrical presentations. This group was accepted by both the aristocratic white society and black society.

A wealthy black woman named Aunt Ciata was a special sponsor of the group and gave parties for Delightful Myrtle at her home. Many of the members of this group, however, also secretly loved to samba, a dance with African roots popular among the poorer population. Eventually, through the support of Aunt Ciata and her friends, samba gained recognition by high society as a respectable form of music and dance.

Members of the group Maracatu perform in the streets of Recife, Brazil, during Carnival in 1999. In Recife, native Indian folklore groups dress in costumes like those worn by their Indian ancestors and dance to the music of native instruments. Reproduced by permission of AP/Wide World Photos.

Beginning of the samba schools

The most important part of modern celebrations in Brazil is the samba schools, which are large neighborhood groups who perform, in costume, a dance called the samba for the gigantic parades during Carnaval. Samba schools began in 1928 in Mangueira (pronounced mon-GAY-ee-rah), a suburb of Rio de Janeiro.

At first, the samba schools were not involved with the mainstream Carnaval celebrations; dances were held in the *favelas,* poor black neighborhoods situated on hillsides around the city and far away from the center of Rio, where the middle and upper classes lived. Samba quickly became so popular, however, that in 1935 authorities allowed it to be a part of Carnaval.

The Brazilian government began giving money to the schools to help pay for costumes and parade floats. Samba schools were formally organized, and by the 1970s, the schools had become year-round entertainment companies that raised money from balls and rehearsals attended by the public. Since then, samba has become world famous. In 1984, the first samba parades were held in the huge Sambadrome, built by Brazilian architect Oscar Niemeyer.

Folklore, Legends, Stories

When the samba schools of Rio de Janeiro choose the themes for their costumes and songs, legends and characters from Afro-Brazilian history and folklore are always among the subjects. One of the most popular folk heroes is Zumbi (pronounced ZOOM-bee), a leader of rebel slaves who jumped off a cliff to keep from being captured by government officials.

Also popular among Brazilian blacks in Rio and in Salvador is a religion with African origins called *candomblé*. Carnaval celebrations in Salvador include groups of dancers known as Afoxé societies, which act out the sacred music and ceremonies of the ancient religion. In another Salvadoran Carnaval tradition, thousands of members of a musical society called the Sons of Gandhi march through the streets dressed in the costume of East African slaves who were shipped to Brazil to work on the plantations.

Carnaval celebrations in the city of Recife, Brazil, are based on the rich folklore traditions of the area, remembered from the days of slavery. Slaves were allowed to elect their own "kings" and other leaders to handle matters within the slave communities on the plantations. A traditional Carnaval dance, the *maracatú*, came from acting out these "coronations," for which the plantation owners sometimes dressed the slave kings in fine clothing and jewelry.

Also in Recife, a native Indian folklore group called the *caboclinhos* dress in costumes like those worn by their Indian ancestors and dance to the music of native instruments that sound like birds singing. This Carnaval group does an intricate dance that tells the story of how the Indians struggled against being overtaken by white colonizers.

Customs, Traditions, Ceremonies

The parade of the samba schools (see "Music, Dance") highlights Carnaval festivities in Rio de Janeiro, but a number of other activities are also traditionally featured throughout the celebration.

Crowning the king

As in other Carnivals throughout the world, Rio de Janeiro crowns a king of Carnaval, who is named King Momo. As Carnaval begins, the mayor of Rio gives King Momo the keys to the city. He then reigns as king for the five days to follow, riding in various parades and making public appearances throughout the festival.

Momo is based on Momus, the Greek god of pranks, and is often costumed as a European king, such as Louis XIV of France. A Carnaval queen and other beauty queens from various areas of the city are also part of the opening ceremonies, in which the "royalty" ride on floats to begin the Carnaval elegance.

Carnaval balls

After the crowning of King Momo, the Carnaval balls begin on Friday night. They are held in major hotels and private clubs each night of Carnaval, with wealthy Brazilians and their guests wearing costumes that cost up to $10,000 each. Some balls are informal, that is, guests may wear casual clothes, or even bathing suits, since these balls are often held at swimming pools. Winners of the best costume awards at the formal balls get their photographs in the newspaper and become well known in Rio.

Street parties that stop traffic

With many people taking a holiday from work, there are street parties during Carnaval from about noon to dawn for the four days of the celebration. Small bands of musicians and samba dancers parade through the neighborhood streets and eventually attract a following of average citizens wearing costumes. These revelers will dance and sing along with the samba group for a few blocks, then stop to rest. Throughout the night, they will join in many mini-parades. This type of party goes on and on, with breaks for eating and drinking in between. The groups sometimes stop traffic; a few streets are even closed to traffic during Carnaval.

The small samba schools and other social groups parade on Friday and Saturday of Carnaval along Rio Branco, a major avenue. Samba groups also gather in their swimwear and hold beach parties in Rio de Janeiro's famous beach district, the Copacabana. These parties are widely covered by television cameras and broadcast throughout the world.

Clothing, Costumes

From the professionally designed costume of a samba dancer to the originality of the average Brazilian enjoying a street party, a Carnaval costume in Brazil is called a *fantasia* (fantasy). Even the very poor save their money all year to have a beautiful fantasia to wear during Carnaval.

Four-hundred-pound Carnival king Momo and the Carnival princess lead the samba parade in Rio de Janeiro, Brazil, in 1997. Momo reigns as king of the city for the five days of Carnival. Reproduced by permission of AP/Wide World Photos.

Samba magic

Samba is famous for its costumes, which are elaborately designed by the creative team of each samba school and carefully made by hundreds of seamstresses who work for months so that the costumes can be delivered just in time for Carnaval. Costumes are designed around the samba schools' theme and are usually short and skimpy, due in part to the hot weather. They are made from fancy, shimmery materials, and are covered with lace, feathers, and sequins. Each costume is worn during only one Carnaval, and the materials are never used to make another costume.

A reveler in Rio de Janeiro, Brazil, during Carnival in 1998. Whether homemade or bought, a Carnival costume requires great effort to make. Reproduced by permission of AP/Wide World Photos.

Afro-Brazilian region of Bahia (Salvador), where the Brazilian Carnaval began.

The most beautiful woman dancer appears as the *porta-bandeira* (pronounced POR-tah bon-DAY-rah) of the school; she wears the costume of an eighteenth-century lady. Every school has a few members who dress in elaborate costumes with high plumes and walk down the street either alone or in small formations.

The *carnavalesco*

Behind the scenes and helping to make each samba school successful in Rio is a talented and intelligent individual called the *carnavalesco,* who helps design, plan, and choreograph the show. Most carnavalescos are well educated in Brazilian folklore and history as well as art and music. They play a big part in choosing the Carnaval theme, designing the costumes, creating characters, and even developing the samba song. They choose costume colors, materials, and details to accurately represent characters and make sure all the dance movements are perfectly coordinated.

He ... or she?

A popular costume tradition during Brazil's Carnaval is to switch gender identities, with men dressing as women and women as men. Such cross-dressers often form large, flashy groups that join in street parades and balls. Some men perfect the look and mannerisms of famous female characters, such as American actress Marilyn Monroe (1926–1962), and hold special shows that are widely attended and televised.

Dressing for the heat—and for safety

Because of the heat and also to avoid having items like jewelry and money

Today, each samba school is allowed to choose its theme, but between 1939 and the late 1960s, Brazilian government dictators chose the themes, which were always based on Brazilian history. Modern themes range from Afro-Brazilian folklore to traditional fairy tales to current world events, but most are on a theme related to Brazil.

Each samba school has a "wing" (small group) of women dancers who wear the traditional costume of the *baianas* (pronounced buy-AH-nahz), or women of the stolen by pickpockets in the crowds, Carnaval spectators dress in the bare minimum. Shorts and bathing suits are commonly worn throughout Carnaval, sometimes even at balls.

Foods, Recipes

A favorite dish during Carnaval in Brazil is called *feijoada* (pronounced fay-hoe-AH-dah), which is a stew made from black beans and different cuts of pork, like bacon, ham, and sausage. Feijoada is a traditional dish that has its roots with the African slaves of Brazil. They were sometimes given leftover pork parts to eat, such as the snout, feet, and tail, and they prepared these parts with beans. Some cooks still use such parts when preparing feijoada.

Feijoada is usually served on Saturdays, including the Saturday before Carnaval, and is served with a rice and tomato dish, greens such as spinach or collards, and perhaps with fried plantains (a banana-like fruit), potatoes, and fried flour made from a starchy tropical root called manioc (pronounced MAN-ee-ahk). Beef is also very popular in Brazil, as are spicy seafood stews flavored with lime and coconut.

A strong, sweetened coffee called *cafezinho* is served everywhere. During Carnaval, people drink great amounts of beer and a sugarcane brandy called *cachaca*. They also enjoy a fruit-based soda called *guarana*.

Arts, Crafts, Games

Everything about Carnaval in Brazil is a work of art, but some of the largest examples of artistic effort are the parade floats of the samba schools. Each school

Fried Plantains

Ingredients

4 to 6 large green plantains
vegetable oil for frying
salt

Directions

1. Peel the plantains and cut them lengthwise into quarters, then cut the quarters in half.
2. Fry on both sides in a large pan in hot oil; younger children should have adult help.
3. When the plantains are golden colored, take them out of the pan and pound them with a wooden kitchen mallet or pestle until they are flat.
4. Return them to the pan and fry them for a few more minutes, until golden brown.
5. Remove plantains from the pan carefully and drain on paper towels. Sprinkle with a little salt.

may have up to four floats to help illustrate its theme. The leading float is called the *abre-alas*. It is the float that introduces the band and its theme, and usually features a design such as a scroll or a window.

The three other floats help the samba school's drama unfold. Each school also presents a beautifully decorated flag each year, embroidered on one side with the school's emblem and on the other with a design related to the year's story.

A parade of floats is the big event on Tuesday evening, the final night of Carnaval. The floats, designed by some of Brazil's most well-known artists and sculptors, parade down the Rio Branco, a major avenue in Rio de Janeiro. Some are true representations of historical events or cultural symbols, and others are funny, cartoonlike illustrations of political or local events. But all are works of art that provide the perfect finishing touch to Carnaval.

Music, Dance

The samba beat is older than Carnaval and comes from West African rhythms that are led with a heavy bass drumbeat. Over time, the music and dances that evolved to the beat came to represent the heart of Carnaval in Rio de Janeiro. The samba schools that were organized around this tradition are now some seventy years old and have become highly respected institutions that are widely supported in Rio. They are generally named for the area of Rio in which the members live, and the groups are very competitive. The thrill of dancing at Carnaval is the event the members look forward to all year.

The *samba-enredo*

The theme song to which each samba school dances is called the *samba-enredo*. The song is usually composed by a member of the school and rehearsed for months by the samba band, which includes a percussion section called the *bateria*. Around Christmas, the songs are recorded and released to the public so that everyone can learn the words and music before Carnaval. When the parade begins, the lead singer, riding on the band's float, sings the song through once and the musicians play the tune. Then everyone begins to sing, and the parade moves toward the Sambadrome (or Sambodromo) for the school's big performance. During the performance, the crowd of spectators joins in the singing.

Dancing the samba

The samba is a fast dance that requires a lot of expert foot and hip movement. From the waist up, however, the dancer keeps his or her body still.

The basic samba move is to step and hop in place with one foot while brushing the other foot across the body. The dancer then steps and hops on the alternate foot, doing at least two complete steps per second. The hips are moved from left to right and right to left as the dancer steps on the right and then the left foot. The upper body, head, and arms are kept facing in the direction the dancer is looking. When the dance step is mastered, the dancer can begin moving the arms by holding them out and ruffling them as a bird ruffles its feathers. A smile is also a part of the dance.

The Sambadrome and samba parades

The Sambadrome in Rio de Janeiro, designed by world-famous architect Oscar Niemeyer, is a huge outdoor arena. It is just under a half-mile long, and can seat 85,000 spectators in tiered seating like that of a football stadium. About 3,000 special reserved seats are at ground level, with tables and bar service. Beneath the stadium are classrooms for samba schools and a Carnaval museum.

The samba parades were once held on only one night, but they went on for eighteen hours or more, so officials decided to divide them into two nights—the Sunday and Monday of Carnaval. Parades start at about 7:30 P.M. on Presidente Vargas Avenue in Rio, and the dancers march to the Sambadrome, where they perform for an hour and a half each. The large samba schools, with as many as 3,500 members per school, are divided into "wings," smaller groups that dance together, each performing one part of the larger story or theme. Samba is said to be like a moving opera.

Those performing at the Sambadrome are the best of the local samba schools, having won regional competitions in the weeks before Carnaval. Some of the same large groups from the poor neighborhoods of Rio are the top competitors every year, and a few have won first place several times. The samba schools are given points on a strict system by judges who watch every move and every detail of the theme and the way it is presented. Points are taken away for even small mistakes. At the end of the competition, each school gets its score, and the one with the highest score wins.

The samba school competition is followed closely by television and radio stations throughout Brazil. Cameras and reporters cover the balls and samba contests leading up to Carnaval, and during the four days of Carnaval, not much else can be seen on TV.

Special Role of Children, Young Adults

Rio de Janeiro devotes one of its three Carnaval days to children, who have their own costume parade. The children's samba schools take to the streets on Saturday, the first day of Carnaval, in glittery new costumes as fancy as those of the adults. The schools have their own children's floats as well. The children parade to the Sambadrome, where they give their performances for large crowds of proud relatives, friends, and the public. Children are watched over carefully in the city, and those without a car ride home are taken home by bus after the parade.

For More Information

Ancona, George. *Carnaval*. New York: Harcourt Brace, 1999.

McKay, Susan. *Brazil: Festivals of the World*. Milwaukee, Wis.: Gareth Stevens, 1997.

Papi, Liza. *Carnavalia! African-Brazilian Folklore and Crafts*. New York: Rizzoli, 1994.

Web sites

"Go Carnaval in Rio." [Online] http://cnn.com/ TRAVEL/DESTINATIONS/9702/rio.carnaval (accessed on January 13, 2000).

Germany

Name of Holiday: Karneval; Fastnacht; Fasching; Fasnet

Introduction

In Germany, the Karneval (pronounced CAR-nay-val) season begins on the eleventh day of the eleventh month at eleven minutes past eleven o'clock in the morning (November 11 at 11:11 A.M.). The reason Karneval is associated with the number eleven is uncertain. Fools and mummers (performers in disguise) in Germany are connected with the number eleven. The number was also used during the early

Participants dressed as witches gather at the traditional Fastnacht event in Waldkirch, a small town in the Black Forest area of Germany, in 1998. In Germany and other countries, traditional costumes are still worn every year during Carnival. Reproduced by permission of AP/Wide World Photos.

1800s by Karneval societies that met to plan the yearly events. The main council of the groups was called the Council of Eleven. According to one of these early planners, the number eleven represented unity and equality because "the right side speaks the same as the left."

Although preparations for Karneval begin on November 11, the Karneval season officially starts the day after Epiphany, January 6, and lasts until midnight on Shrove Tuesday, the day before Lent begins. Karneval in Germany is a time of true merriment; it is called the Fifth Season, or Season of Fools.

History

In Germany during the thirteenth and fourteenth centuries, groups of young men held a rite to welcome spring and entertain their neighbors after a long, hard winter. They dressed in sheep– or goatskins, wore their hair and beards long, and ran through the countryside talking gibberish and behaving wildly. This custom became known as Fastnacht (pronounced FAHS-nockt) or Fasnet (pronounced FAHS-net), meaning "night of the fast." It is also translated as "nonsense night."

In some areas of Germany, the custom was called Schembartlauf, meaning "run of the hairy men." This strange festival was abolished by local governments in 1339, but it was brought back in 1349 by members of a butchers' guild. Wealthy young men later adopted the tradition.

During the 1400s, the "hairy men" became known as "fools." They made it a game to poke fun at society during a time when life in Germany, and most of Europe, was difficult because so many had died from a terrible plague called the Black Death.

Fools' societies were organized in Europe's large cities, in the homes of noblemen, and later in small towns. These societies became widespread from the fifteenth through the seventeenth centuries. They brought back old pre-Lenten festival customs, and made fun of their neighbors and of society with a form of noisy, foolish behavior called *charivari* (pronounced kah-ree-VAH-ree). They also held large parades featuring floats designed to make fun of people's foolish pride.

During the 1600s, the wealthy added masked balls and carriage promenades to Karneval celebrations. When Europeans immigrated to the Americas, they brought the tradition and festivals of the fool with them, where they eventually became part of Carnival celebrations in North and South America and the Caribbean.

In 1794, the French occupied the Rhineland region of Germany, the region along the river Rhine, and banished the fools' societies and Karneval celebrations. Although the ban was lifted in 1801, the societies were no longer organized and events were poorly planned. By the mid-1800s, the wealthy people of the cities controlled most of the festivities, and they introduced many Karneval traditions that are still in place today.

Glamour and folklore

As Carnival celebrations grew in European cities such as Venice, Italy, the German cities of Nuremberg and Munich began to adopt some of the glamour of the Venetian Carnevale. In the late 1800s, a Fasching (pronounced FAH-sching; foolish) society was formed in Munich to plan fancy dress balls and large parades. A prince and princess of fools were chosen, and they wore jeweled crowns and furs.

Today, local Karneval clubs plan and carry out activities in many parts of Germany. The clubs are usually run by men, who in some areas dress in fancy soldiers' uniforms. In Cologne, as many as forty different Karneval clubs organize the festivities.

In the Black Forest region of southwestern Germany, the "hairy man" custom continued during the 1700s. Young men put on red rags and big bells, and they ran and leaped, hitting people and beating the ground. During the nineteenth century, a revival of German folklore brought about renewed Karneval celebrations in the countryside. When the French took control of Germany after World War I (1914–18), they banned Karneval, but the Germans secretly formed fools' societies to keep their Karneval customs alive.

After World War II (1939–45), celebrations were again held throughout the Black Forest region, with large crowds of tourists coming to see the old-style costumes and parades. Karneval, or Fasnet, is

The Cologne–Warringen Carnival prince kisses his bride outside of city hall in 1996.
Carnival guards sometimes dress like soliders in Napoleon's army.
Reproduced by permission of AP/Wide World Photos.

still held as a popular celebration of German folklore in this region today.

Folklore, Legends, Stories

Karneval celebrations throughout Germany are steeped in legend and folklore. Folktales that originate in various parts of the country, however, contain elements that are unique to a region's history.

The waking and killing of Karneval

A strange character called Hoppeditz represents Karneval in some parts of Germany. He is a puppet or a straw man who is said to rise from his bed, or grave, at 11:11 A.M. on November 11, the beginning of Karneval. When Karneval is over, townspeople drag him through the streets or cart him off in a wheelbarrow and burn or bury him, representing the killing of Karneval in preparation for Lent.

Battle of winter and spring

In Saxony (northern Germany), a battle between winter and spring has been fought during Karneval since the thirteenth century, with individuals dressed in costumes to represent the dueling seasons. Spring always wins, and winter is sometimes burned in effigy, a crude figure made to represent a person who is disliked or hated, after his defeat by Dame Sun.

German Karneval plays

The fools' societies that were popular in Europe during the fifteenth through the seventeenth centuries developed a type of play called the *sottie*. The sottie was a comedy in which the actors and theme centered around the fool, whose role was to poke fun at humanity.

A Karneval play called the Shrovetide play also became popular during this time and is considered Germany's first nonreligious play. The most well-known writer of these early plays was Hans Sachs (1494–1576). Shrovetide plays were usually performed by amateurs.

Child eater and fool gobbler

Two folklore figures that developed from the characters of the fool and the wild man in German Karneval parades of the sixteenth century were the "child eater" and the "fool gobbler." These folk figures were portrayed as evil giants who walked about villages collecting "bad" children or fools and gobbling them up.

On board the Ship of Fools

German poet Sebastian Brant (c. 1458–1521) wrote *Ship of Fools* (*Das Narrenschiff*) in 1494 after watching a Karneval parade in Nuremberg, Germany. His account was inspired by the Karneval's main float, which was designed as a ship of fools.

The book was translated into several languages, and its theme was again made popular in the twentieth century by Ameri-

A clown holds balloons during a 1998 Carnival parade in Wasungen, Germany, the site of one of the oldest traditional carnivals in eastern Germany. Many German cities feature fools' processions, large parades with hundreds of fools, jesters, and clowns. Reproduced by permission of AP/Wide World Photos.

can writer Katherine Anne Porter (1890–1980) with her novel *Ship of Fools* (1962). Porter's novel was made into a movie of vignettes (pronounced vin-YETS; short scenes in a film) about people on an ocean voyage who face many frustrations.

Customs, Traditions, Ceremonies

Karneval festivities in Germany, like Carnival celebrations in other countries,

"Mardi-Gras" (West Germany)

Come and join the Carnival
   Carnival
      Carnival
Come and join the Carnival,
all the people say!

Blow your trumpet
  wear your hat
and if you are
  thin or fat
who is there
  to care for that?
The clowns are down
  our way!
Singing, dancing,
feasting, vaulting,
stamping, laughing,
somersaulting....
Come and join the Carnival,
it's Mardi-Gras today!

—*Jean Kenward*

Source: Let's Celebrate, *compiled by John Foster. Oxford: Oxford University Press, 1989, p. 21.*

include such traditions as crowning of a king and queen, the staging of elaborate parades and processions, and general feasting and merriment. Other customs are uniquely German and stem from regional folklore and traditions.

Fools' processions

Many German cities feature fools' processions, large parades with hundreds of fools, jesters, and clowns. In the Black Forest region of Germany, the fools who participate in the Karneval parade are dressed in red like devils. The event is held on the Sunday before Ash Wednesday, beginning at noon with loud music. Everyone pokes fun at everyone else, and those who take the jesting in good humor get candy, fruit, and flowers. There is a big bonfire in the evening to end the festivities.

Prince and princess of Karneval

Every German town crowns its own prince and princess of Karneval. In Cologne, Prince Karneval is called "His Crazy Highness." The prince and princess and their court are allowed to live at City Hall all day on Shrove Tuesday, the day before Lent begins. They are in charge of the city government for the day and are attended by a Fool's Court, whose members wear pointed caps and badges proclaiming their membership in the Order of Fools.

The royal couple's guards sometimes dress like soldiers in Napoleon's army, which controlled the Rhineland region of Germany from about 1800 to 1815. These costumed soldiers carry wooden rifles and poke fun at the military.

The day women take over

The Women's Karneval began in 1824, when overworked washerwomen in a small village near Bonn, Germany, decided to take over the town hall and declare a day off for themselves. They crowned a "washing princess" and claimed a women's day, which quickly became an annual tradition. This tradition continues today, as women—costumed as witches, devils, clowns, soldiers, and other characters—storm the Bonn town hall and take charge of the city for the day.

Women's Day is celebrated all over Germany on the Thursday before Lent beginning at 11:11 A.M. Women do all sorts of crazy things, like running through the cobblestone streets, cutting off men's ties and giving them a kiss on the cheek in return for the snippings. Parades are held, featuring hundreds of floats, with everyone in costume. People riding on the floats throw candy and flowers to the crowd. At night, women go to nightclubs without their husbands or boyfriends for a fun and rowdy "girls' night out."

Rose Monday Parade in Cologne

The highlight of Karneval in Cologne, Dusseldorf, and Mainz, Germany, is the Rose Monday Parade. The parade in Cologne is the largest in Europe. It starts at 11:11 A.M. on the Monday before Ash Wednesday and features floats, bands, and groups of people masquerading as fools. More than seven thousand people and three hundred horses participate in this procession. Those riding on floats throw candy into the crowd lined up along the streets to watch the parade.

Karneval in Munich

Karneval in Munich, Germany, begins on January 7. Throughout the season, until Ash Wednesday, the city sparkles with hundreds of costume balls and parties. The final week of Karneval is the wildest. Partygoers fill the nightclubs and drink beer until the early morning hours. A parade called Mad Munich (München Harrisch) is held on the Sunday before Ash Wednesday and features floats and costumes like those worn in Venice, Italy, during the 1500s and 1600s.

Every seven years—1998 is the most recent—the Munich Schafflers, makers of wooden casks, perform a special dance through the streets during Karneval to commemorate the end of the Black Death, a terrible disease that killed thousands of Germans during the 1300s and 1400s.

As Karneval draws to a close, a final costume ball is held. At midnight before Ash Wednesday, the "fool" representing Karneval is put into a fake coffin and carried out of the city, followed by a crowd of people sloshing the last of their beer at him. A street sweeper comes behind, symbolically sweeping away the trash of another year's madness.

Clothing, Costumes

Outlandish costumes are an essential part of German Karneval parades, processions, and balls. Many balls are theme based and are open to anyone wearing the theme clothing, which can mean anything from striped underwear and dunce caps to formal evening gowns, black ties, and tuxedos.

Clown costumes are a favorite at the German Karneval in Cologne. People also wear fools' caps, or *kappen*. During the costume balls in Munich, masqueraders often wear costumes that were typical of the splendor of the elaborate balls held in Venice, Italy, during the 1500s and 1600s.

In other towns in southern Germany, Karneval is celebrated by disguised fools who run through town making mischief. In Schuddig, the fools wear red-fringed clothes, traditional masks, and big hats decorated with snail shells. As they run through the streets, they hit people

A masked reveler uses a six-foot stick to perform the Fool's Jump during Carnival in Rottweil, Germany, in 1997. In Rottweil, the Fool's Jump costumes are often decorated with chicken feathers. Reproduced by permission of AP/Wide World Photos.

Foods, Recipes

Fastnachtkuchen (pronounced FAHS-nockt-coo-ken), fried doughnuts coated with sugar, are especially popular during Karneval in Germany. They are similar to the pancakes made in Great Britain on Shrove Tuesday.

Other popular Karneval foods in Germany are eggs, pretzels, sausages, pickled herring, snails, and homemade noodles. Legend has it that German bakers made pretzels to represent the crossed arms of a Christian at prayer, with the palms of his hands on opposite shoulders. This makes the pretzel an appropriate food for Lent.

Arts, Crafts, Games

Karneval is a time for artistic talents to shine, especially when it comes to creating the large and elaborate floats featured in many parades. For the Rose Monday parades, special tractor-and-trailer floats display life-size paper figures of real celebrities, politicians, and other public figures, who are made fun of during the parade. These works of art take months to design and complete.

with inflated hogs' bladders, an old custom that has lost its significance over time.

In Rottweil, the costumes for the Fool's Jump (Narrensprung) are hand painted or decorated with chicken feathers. The masks are strange, even frightening, and some are decorated with foxtails. During the parade, marchers wear eighty-pound sets of bells that keep up a rhythm to their step. A huge, costumed "rooster" tries to pick up pretty girls and take them away.

Music, Dance

Music groups and dance groups called *buettenredner* (pronounced BUE-ten-red-ner) that mock political figures and everyday life perform during German Karneval shows called "sessions." The Buettenredner are ordinary people, not professional singers and dancers, and the shows can be quite funny. The crowd is also encouraged to sing along.

The groups originated with people making "washtub speeches" ridiculing the

Berlin Pancakes or Shrove Tuesday Cakes

Ingredients

2 cups plus 2 tablespoons flour

½ ounce yeast

dash of salt

3½ tablespoons sugar

1 cup plus 2¼ teaspoons milk

3 eggs, separated

7 tablespoons butter

1 teaspoon vanilla extract

apricot or other jam

oil for frying

powdered sugar for sprinkling

Directions

1. Make a soft dough by combining the flour, yeast, salt, sugar, milk, egg yolks, butter, and vanilla extract. Cover with a towel and let rise.

2. Roll out the dough on a lightly floured surface to about 1/3 inch thick. Divide the rectangular dough in half and set one half aside.

3. Use the rim of a drinking glass to lightly mark 8 circles on one half of the dough (circles should be about 3½ inches in circumference). Put a spoonful of jam in the center of each circle.

4. Trace the outline of each circle with a thin coating of egg white. Gently place the other half of the dough over the dough with the jam rings. Press down lightly so that the dollops of jam do not spread.

5. Using the rim of the glass, cut through both pieces of dough to cut out the circles. Press the edges of the dough together to seal the top and bottom halves.

6. Cover the circles with a towel and let rise again, about 10 minutes.

7. Heat oil in a deep fryer and place a few Berliners at a time into hot oil. Cover and let cook for about 5 minutes. Turn the doughnuts and continue cooking until golden brown, about 10 minutes total.

8. Remove with a slotted spoon and drain on a paper towel. Sprinkle with powdered sugar.

political establishment during the early 1800s. Anyone who wanted to could stand on top of an upside-down washtub and make up verses about town officials or other public figures. This type of political ridicule remains a central part of Karneval celebrations in Germany.

Special Role of Children, Young Adults

School is out for most German children on Shrove Tuesday. As part of the celebration they make or buy costumes similar to those children in the United States wear on Halloween: cowboys, pirates, and robbers. They may also paint their faces for Karneval.

As in Brazil, the Saturday before Ash Wednesday is the day for children's parades, which feature floats and costumes just like those in the adults' parades. The most famous of these is in Mainz. In the children's parades, a young prince and princess of Karneval ride on floats and throw sweets to the crowd.

For More Information

Germany: Festivals of the World. Milwaukee, Wis.: Gareth Stevens Publishing, 1997.

Russ, Jennifer M. *German Festivals and Customs.* London: Oswald Wolff, 1982.

Web sites

"Binche's Carnival." [Online] http://www.geocities. com/Paris/4728/carnival.html (accessed on January 18, 2000).

"Fasching." [Online] http://www.bavaria.com/enter-tainment/ fasching_us.html (accessed on January 18, 2000).

Italy

Name of Holiday: Carnevale

Introduction

Although the Carnevale (pronounced kar-nay-VAL) in Venice is the most well known, Italy has at least a dozen major celebrations, each of them unique and based on the history and culture of the city or town where it is held. Celebrations may begin shortly after Christmas and continue until Ash Wednesday, although the biggest are held during the week before Lent. Carnevale week in Italy is called *settimana grassa,* or "fat week." Costuming, parades, music, feasting—and food fights—are at the heart of these festivals.

History

Because Rome was the center of early Christianity, some of the first Carnevale celebrations were held in Italy, during the Middle Ages (c. A.D. 500–1500). Early writings show that people had begun to celebrate the festival by 1140; by the 1300s, Carnevale was becoming more and more popular; and by the 1400s and 1500s, the celebration reached its height. In the city of Venice, people celebrated for six months, but the peak of the party was from mid-January, when meat was most plentiful, to Ash Wednesday, when Lent began and eating meat was prohibited by Church law.

Early Italian Carnevale celebrations centered around eating and drinking, gambling, wearing masks, singing, and dancing. Throwing flour, eggs, and oranges at masked paraders in a kind of crazy battle was another form of Carnevale revelry.

By the late 1600s, people began throwing confetti made from sugar-coated almonds or plaster pellets. Revelers sometimes used slings to make sure they hit their targets. During the 1700s and 1800s, people celebrating Carnevale had to wear wire face masks to keep from being hit by oranges, confetti, and flowers.

The Romans of the late 1700s celebrated Shrove Tuesday, the final day of Carnevale, with a citywide candlelight procession. Each individual held a lit candle and tried to blow out the candles of the persons around him while shouting, "Death to anyone who is not carrying a candle!" No one was allowed to move from the spot where he stood, but he could relight his candle if someone blew it out.

Carnevale celebrations began in the city of Viareggio (pronounced vee-ah-REJ-oh) in 1873 with a procession of decorated floats on the main street. Citizens who felt their taxes were too high decided to join in the fun. They put on masks to keep from being recognized and marched in the parade, shouting rude and humorous comments about the town tax collector. This form of making fun of political and other public figures continues to this day in the Viareggio Carnevale parades.

Carnevale was very popular in the city of Venice; in 1687, some thirty thousand visitors came to celebrate. The wealthy held magnificent costume balls and noblemen paraded in the streets in disguises that featured gold, silver, and jewels. The middle classes and the poor put on masks and costumes also, and everyone walked up and down the square. There was plenty of wine to drink and a lot of food to eat. As a Carnevale sport from the 1600s to about 1800, people chased bulls through the narrow streets of the city.

As the years went by, masked parades became less common, but Venetians still held costume balls. When the Italian dictator Benito Mussolini (1883–1945) outlawed masks and finally Carnevale itself, Venice did not celebrate for many years. In 1979, the festival was revived, and since then, it has come back in all its glittering, costumed glory.

Folklore, Legends, Stories

Each of Italy's Carnevales has its own history and folklore, and each traditional mask has a character behind it with a story to tell. All of these are part of the country's long Carnevale heritage, which gives Italians of today a lot to choose from when dressing in costume or designing parade floats.

The Miller's Daughter: Leader of a rebellion

Famous in the folklore of Ivrea, Italy, is Violetta, the Miller's Daughter, a girl of the twelfth century. Her story begins on her wedding night, when she was forced to sleep with the local landowner as a form of tax he had placed on marriage. Once she was alone with the landowner in his castle, she took out a knife she had hidden in her clothing and stabbed him. Then she cut off his head, held it up to the window for the villagers to see, and threw it into the river. Violetta then set fire to the castle. After three days of fighting the landowner's men, the people won their freedom.

To this day, the Miller's Daughter, or La Mugnaia (pronounced lah moon-YI-ah), plays an important role in Carnevale celebrations in Ivrea. She is the star of a big, torchlit parade on the Saturday night before Ash Wednesday, when a girl dressed as her character rides on a parade float, attended by lords and ladies in medieval costumes. Soldiers and a general in French uniform representing the era of Napoleon, who once captured the region, ride by her side. Also in the parade are knights in armor, flag bearers, and other characters important in Italy's history. Parties throughout the city begin after the parade, and people stay up all night, moving in groups from one party to another.

The next day, the Miller's Daughter and the general arrive for the city's big bean feast, where La Mugnaia serves bowls of delicious beans to the crowd. Afterward, the town's mayor throws a brick from the ancient castle into the river, just as the Miller's Daughter threw the landowner's head into the river hundreds of years before.

La Mugnaia is also a leading figure in putting Carnevale in Ivrea to rest. On Shrove Tuesday, she gives the cue for the burning of the poles that signal the end of the year's festival (see "Customs, Traditions, Ceremonies").

Customs, Traditions, Ceremonies

Carnevale in Italy has been celebrated for centuries by the poor and the wealthy, by old and young, in small villages and in the grand ballrooms of Venice. Over time, they have grown into elaborate celebrations filled with traditions both old and new.

Parades and processions

In Venice during the seventeenth and eighteenth centuries, one of the favorite Carnevale activities was to dress in costume and walk back and forth along a street called Campo Santo Stefano, and in later years, around the larger San Marco Square. Crowds of both rich and poor people, everyone disguised by masks and in Carnevale dress, participated in this activity. The term for it was *fare le vasche,* which means "swim in the pool." The term describes the back-and-forth movement of the crowd in the streets.

In modern Venice, a big public party is held in San Marco Square on Fat Tuesday, with concerts featuring international music. Fireworks complete the big open-air ball. Venice is famous for its gondolas, which are long, narrow boats that are guided by boatmen called gondoliers. On Fat Tuesday, the gondolas carry celebrities in costume, lovers, and tourists along the Grand Canal, who watch the fireworks display over the water.

The Carnevale parade is a long-standing tradition in Italy, and each city has its own unique form. In Viareggio, colorful floats carry figures of current politicians, entertainers, or intellectuals made from papier-mâché. These are created by float designers who work all year on the projects. The figures have moving arms, legs, mouths, and eyes to make them look as real as possible. The object of the parade is usually to make fun of these prominent people, or make a statement about them that is popular with the citizens. Children and teenagers throw confetti and shooting stars into the crowd from each float.

The city of Putignano (pronounced poo-tee-NYAH-noh) has a similar parade, also with papier-mâché characters riding on floats. This city has many festivities leading up to Carnevale. One is a very old tradition called *ndondaro* (pronounced nyon-DAH-roh), in which a procession of people dressed as peasants, warriors, and other characters from Italy's history parade through town playing very noisy home-made instruments.

In the town of Bosa, citizens in costume parade through the streets, acting out skits that make fun of their fellow citizens. The townspeople also march in white robes and carry lanterns during Carnevale. In Ronciglione, horses and riders play an important part in Carnevale parades.

Masked balls

Venice, especially, is famous for its masked balls, which are held for ten days during Carnevale at many different locations. These balls are glamorous parties, sometimes held at old castles, with music and dancing. Everyone dresses in the most magnificent costumes—often these are traditional costumes from the eighteenth century. During the last five days of Carnevale, the wealthy play host to famous people from all over Europe who come for the masquerades.

Sports and games

Carnevale in Italy has for centuries been a time for unusual sports and games. During the 1700s in Venice, acrobats built human pyramids outside the palace of the chief city official. They also performed a stunt called "flight of the angel," in which one acrobat slid down a rope from the top of a tall building and handed a bouquet of flowers to the city official. The "flight of the dove" entertained the crowds when a paper dove slid down a rope from the bell tower, spilling confetti on the streets all the way. City street sweepers held wheelbarrow races.

Chasing bulls through the narrow streets was also popular during the seventeenth and eighteenth centuries; any bull chaser who was in danger from an angry animal could jump into a canal to get out of the way. Crowds gathered to watch the spectacle and, after the excitement was over, they feasted in the square until midnight.

In modern-day Oristano, citizens reenact a jousting tournament of the Middle Ages (c. A.D. 500–1500). Horsemen cos-

Gondolas carry passengers beneath the Bridge of Sighs in Venice, Italy. On Fat Tuesday, the gondolas along the Grand Canal carry celebrities in costume, lovers, and tourists who watch the fireworks display over the water. Reproduced by permission of Susan D. Rock.

tumed as knights spur their horses to a gallop and then try to thrust their swords into a swinging star-shaped object. This tournament is called the Sartigilia (pronounced sar-tee-EEL-yah).

Food fight in Ivrea

The town of Ivrea has one of Italy's most unusual Carnevale customs—throwing oranges. The people of Ivrea don't just throw them, however; they do battle with them. On the Sunday, Monday, and Tuesday of

Carnevale week, some sixty tons of blood oranges, shipped by train to Ivrea from Sicily, are hurled toward the buildings surrounding the piazzas, or open town squares. "Soldiers" on foot defend the buildings from the squadrons passing by in horse-drawn carts.

The teams throw the juicy fruit at one another with a vengeance, penetrating edges of the armorlike helmets and padded guards the fighters wear. Anyone who does not want to participate in the battle of oranges must wear a red knit cap like that worn by French revolutionaries. Therefore, most of the town is decked out in their red-cap "costumes" during these three days of Carnevale. Many Ivreans go back to work on Wednesday with bumps and bruises to show for their "bravery." Juice and orange peels are everywhere, filling the air with their fragrance and the streets with their slippery sugar.

Oranges have played an important role in Italian history. The country has been invaded at least twice by conquerors hoping to gain control of the orchards producing these "golden apples of the gods."

Killing Carnevale

In Ivrea, the end of Carnevale is marked by a ceremony of fire. Carnevale is represented by five tall poles called *scarli,* which have greenery made of juniper and heather wound around them all the way to the top. On the Monday before Ash Wednesday, the most recently married couple from each of five neighborhoods digs up the first shovelful of soil from the spot where the neighborhood scarli will be set in the ground.

On Tuesday evening, the Miller's Daughter (La Mugnaia) and her compan-

ion, the general, arrive in the central piazza. She draws her sword and holds it high in the air as a signal for young boys to begin torching the greenery wrapped around the central scarli. As it burns, everyone watches closely, for if the flames reach the flag at the top of the pole it means good luck and many marriages for the neighborhood in the coming year.

The crowd then walks to the other four neighborhoods to burn the remaining scarli as a flute player plays a sad tune for the "funeral" of Carnevale. When all the scarli have burned, the general drags his sword over the pavement, leading a quiet procession that signifies the death of the festival for another year and the coming of the solemn season of Lent.

In the city of Putignano, King Carnevale is given a mock funeral on the afternoon of Fat Tuesday, the last day of the festival. He is carried through the city in a coffin, with his "wife" walking beside him, crying and naming all the good things about him. A long line of women mourners walk behind her, chanting and wailing. When the procession is over, the coffin is burned to mark the end of Carnevale.

An early twentieth century custom in Brescia seems almost cruel. Straw figures of an old woman were stuffed with firecrackers and hung from balconies all over town. Then in the evening, a match was struck to set the "old women" on fire, one at a time, so that people could walk around and see them. As the fire burned, the firecrackers were set off, and the old woman's limbs flew off in all directions as they exploded in each part of the figure. The children especially loved this custom, appropriately called "Burning the Old Woman."

Clothing, Costumes

Like other countries that celebrate Carnival, Italy has its traditional masks and costumes that have been worn by celebrants for centuries, each with its own story and personality based on a real or fictional character. These masks are especially important in the city of Venice, where dressing in costumes has been a major part of Carnevale for hundreds of years.

The masks and the characters behind them

Italian comedy theater of the sixteenth to eighteenth centuries—known as the *commedia dell'arte* (pronounced kom-AID-ee-uh del-AR-tay)—created some of the most famous characters in Italian costume. Among them is Harlequin, the silly but crafty clown with his multicolored suit. Another is Punchinello, a hunchback with a tall white hat, white baggy trousers and nightshirt, and black mask with a large, hooked nose. Punchinello became the famous puppet character Punch in the Punch and Judy puppet shows.

Pierrot (pronounced pyair-ROW), a sad clown wearing an oversized coat, is another famous costume character from the commedia dell'arte. The French adapted this character for their Carnival, and he later became the fierce fighter Pierrot Grenade (pronounced greh-NOD) of Caribbean Carnival.

In Venice, one of the most popular traditional costumes is that of La Bautta (the Domino). The domino costume includes a white mask, a black silk hood, a black cape, and a three-cornered black hat. Il Dottore is another popular character. He is a professor or doctor of law and wears a long black gown and a stern-looking black mask.

These, and other costumes, allowed people to go to places they did not normally go, and do things they would not ordinarily be permitted to do, because their identity was completely hidden. Certain groups of maskers could be identified, however, by a particular item they wore. For example, the "stocking" groups all wore colorfully patterned stockings.

The official mask for the Viareggio Carnevale is that of Burlamacco, a clown who borrows bits of costume from other clowns. He wears checkered overalls, a white pompon, a red headband, and a black cloak.

In Putignano, a favorite mask is that of the *farinella,* or court jester. This costume has multicolored patchwork overalls and a pointed hat and shoes with bells on the ends. Farinella was a simple food eaten by poor people in the countryside. It was made from chickpeas and toasted barley.

Nontraditional costumes

Today, Italians who do not want to wear a traditional Carnevale costume may dress as anything they choose. Some put on the costume of people of other trades, old and new, such as woodcutters, bakers, or police officers. Others dress as animals, peasants, monsters, extraterrestrial visitors, or as characters of their own creation. The Carnevale tradition of men dressing as women, and women as men, applies in modern Italy as well.

Walking the streets in costume has always been a favorite Carnevale activity in Venice, and today large groups of students often dress alike in the same costume and take the train downtown, where they dance in the streets and give short performances in cafes.

Foods, Recipes

Feasting traditions have been carried on for centuries in Italy, which is well known for its deliciously prepared foods. Today, food plays as big a part as ever in Italian Carnevale celebrations. From beans to rich stews, from fish to fried pastries, everyone seems to eat well at this time of year.

Fat Tuesday, the day before Lent begins and the day when the most elaborate meals are prepared, is called Marte dì Grasso (pronounced mar-TAY dee-GRAH-soh) in Italian. A traditional Fat Tuesday feast consists of numerous pork dishes, a bean stew with leeks and potatoes, fried polenta (cooked cornmeal), cabbage, stuffed pasta, garbanzo bean soup, cheese pie, pumpkin pie, and sugary fritters.

Beans and chocolates

Once a year, wealthy landowners in Ivrea used to distribute free beans to the poor farmers who worked their fields. But the beans did not help the workers' hunger the rest of the year, so one year the farmers threw the beans back at the landowners for spite. This is said to be the beginning of the food-throwing tradition in Ivrea. Later, in 1872, wealthy citizens threw beans, oranges, and candy to the poor during Carnevale, supplying them with extra food to live on during the year.

In recent times, beans have become the favorite Carnevale dish of the people of Ivrea. Bean feasts are held throughout the city for three weeks during the Carnevale season, but the biggest feast of all is held on Carnevale Saturday night and Sunday morning. During the feast, some thirty-five big pots of a special bean dish called *tofeja* (pronounced toe-FAY-hah)—named for the short, four-handled terra-cotta pot it was once cooked in—are simmered over fires on the city's main piazza. The cooking begins on Saturday night, and people start coming to sample the beans around two or three o'clock in the morning on Sunday. The serving begins early Sunday morning.

Tofeja is made from butter beans or cannellini beans cooked with pork sausage, pork fat, and spareribs or other cuts of pork. Local farmers usually donate the beans and pork cuts. The poor of Ivrea come to the big bean feast for a delicious meal, and afterward they are treated to chocolates and cheeses. The hosts of the feast also serve red wine.

The Miller's Daughter of Carnevale fame and the French general who rides in the parade with her come to the bean feast on Sunday morning. After sampling the tofeja and drinking a toast, the Miller's Daughter begins serving bowls of beans to the poor. She and the general are cheered by the townspeople.

Fried "lies" and "nuns' ribbons"

Because Carnival in Italy was traditionally a time for using up the eggs, butter, and other spoilable foodstuffs in the household before Lent, fried pastries, pancakes, and other such treats have always been a part of pre-Lenten celebrations.

Light, sugary, fried ribbons of dough are served in nearly every town that celebrates Carnevale. The only variations are the different liqueurs (sweet alcoholic beverages flavored with ingredients such as

Potato Gnocchi

Ingredients

4 large baking potatoes

1 teaspoon salt

1 to 1½ cups all-purpose flour

1 egg

10 cups water

1 stick unsalted butter

fresh sage leaves

1 cup grated Parmesan cheese

Directions

1. Bake the potatoes, then peel them while they are still warm.

2. Mash the peeled potatoes and add the salt, egg, and as much of the flour as it takes to make a smooth, thick paste.

3. Roll the potato mixture into logs about ½ inch in width, and cut the logs into 1-inch pieces. Press the traditional gnocchi pattern into the pieces by rolling them lightly over a cheese grater.

4. Bring the water to a boil in a large pot and cook the gnocchi 1 to 3 minutes or until they rise to the top of the water.

5. Melt the butter in a small saucepan and add the crushed sage leaves.

6. When each gnocchi is done, take it out of the water with a slotted spoon, then drain it and serve it with the melted sage butter or with pasta sauce if you prefer. Sprinkle Parmesan cheese on top.

orange or almond) with which the cooks flavor them—and the odd names they go by. They are called "little lies" in the Piedmont; "rags" in Tuscany; "lettuces" in Emilia-Romagna; "gossips" in Milan; and "nuns' ribbons" in many other Italian towns.

Another Carnevale favorite is *frittelle*, fritters of dough sprinkled with sugar and filled with fruit and nuts. They have given their name to the expression *fare le frittelle* (pronounced far lay free-TAY-lay), which means "have a good time" at Carnevale.

Salt cod and onions

Salt cod is an important Carnevale dish in Ivrea, Italy. The fish is served on Ash Wednesday as a last feast before the beginning of Lent. It is soaked for four days, and 175 pounds of onions are sliced to cook with it. A red and a white sauce are prepared, and then on Tuesday night, the fish is fried, taking all night and part of Wednesday morning. It is layered with the onions and sauce to make a main dish that is served with polenta. Everyone in town comes to eat, and they bring dishes in which to take food home. Months later, they may take the fish from their freezer and dine again, remembering the chilly Carnevale night when it was first prepared.

Gnocchi Friday

In the city of Verona, Italy, the last Friday of Carnevale has a parade devoted entirely to food. Leading the parade is *gnocchi* (pronounced NYOH-key), the delicious potato-and-flour dish that has been called the symbol of Carnevale in Italy. Once made from only flour and water, this poor man's dish was served free to the citizens during Carnevale.

Today—after the Carnevale parade in which Il Papa del Gnocco (the Pope of Gnocchi) rides on a float with an enormous forkful of gnocchi for a scepter—gnocchi, sausages, and polenta with herring are served to all in the piazza.

Arts, Crafts, Games

As with Carnival everywhere, the art of float and costume design is important in Italy. Venice is especially famous for its beautiful masks. Venetian masks worn with costumes were traditionally created to cover the entire face of the wearer so that the person's identity would not be revealed. Some of the masks are made from porcelain, and are so elaborate and delicate that they are meant only for display as wall hangings.

Copies of the eighteenth-century costumes worn by the wealthy are often made from gorgeous silks, satins, and laces in purple, blue, gold, silver, black, and white. Because it is still winter at Carnevale time, the skimpy, revealing costumes of South America and the Caribbean are not worn in Italy. Instead, the costumes are long, full, and magnificent. The commedia dell'arte costumes are designed just like those of the early theater, in a brilliant jumble of colors and fine fabrics.

Music, Dance

Carnevale is a time for music in Italy, as it is in other countries. In Venice, the Casino di Venezi features classical music concerts. A public party and concert is held in San Marco Square, with music from many countries and cultures.

For More Information

Berg, Elizabeth. *Italy: Festivals of the World*. Milwaukee, Wis.: Gareth Stevens, 1997.

Calvino, Italo. *Italian Folktales*. New York: Harcourt Brace, 1990.

Rowen, Shirley, and David Rowen. *Carnival in Venice*. New York: Harry N. Abrams, 1989.

Trinidad and Tobago

Name of Holiday: Carnival

Introduction

Trinidad and Tobago is an independent nation made up of two islands in the Caribbean Sea just off the northeast coast of Venezuela. Because they are so near the equator, these islands have summerlike weather year-round, so Carnival is a hot-weather celebration at which the crowd wears shorts and swimsuits.

Carnival in Trinidad and Tobago is one of the largest and most popular Carnivals in the world. The main celebration is held in Port-of-Spain, Trinidad, the nation's capital. Carnival is sometimes called Mas (pronounced MOSS) in Trinidad. Mas is a short word for "masquerade," and dressing in costume for Carnival is called "playing mas."

Like the population of Trinidad and Tobago, Carnival is a mixture of European, East Indian, Caribbean, Asian, and African cultures that, in part, is said to represent the joy of freedom after many years of slavery. Trinidadians have an expression that refers to this cultural mix and to the equality of all people at Carnival time: "All Ah We Is One."

History

When French planters were allowed to settle in Spanish-ruled Trinidad beginning in 1783, they brought to the island their holiday custom of masquerading in the streets and holding masked balls. This partylike atmosphere was carried on from Christmas to Ash Wednesday. The French aristocrats dressed in costume and were followed by musicians as they visited the homes of friends, stopping to eat, drink, and make merry.

The Indian natives preferred their own cultural customs and did not choose to participate in the masking. The free black people on the island were allowed to celebrate Carnival only if they kept their activities apart from those of the French. The black slaves brought to work on Trinidad's plantations from French-speaking colonies on other Caribbean islands and from Africa sometimes held their own Carnival, dressing in homemade costumes and imitating

the French but also celebrating with traditional African rituals.

In 1834, when slavery ended on the island, the freed slaves held their Carnival in the streets. These early Carnivals were rowdy, often with stick fighting, torch carrying, loud drumming, and nearly nude parading. Among the first costumed bands were those imitating the military bands that had been appointed by the British to maintain order during the Christmas and Carnival seasons.

Many people from the East Indies and from China came to Trinidad and Tobago to work on the plantations after the abolition of slavery, and they added elements of their cultures to Carnival. The British, who had taken Trinidad from the Spanish in 1797, did not approve of the Carnival celebrations and tried to ban them. This resulted in riots in 1881 that convinced the British that Carnival was an important part of the island's culture and should be allowed to continue.

After World War II (1939–45), the Trinidad Carnival grew tremendously, taking on most of the characteristics it has today. By the time Trinidad and Tobago won its independence from England in 1962, Carnival had become a well-established island tradition.

Today, the Trinidad and Tobago Carnival, more than two hundred years old, is known throughout the world and loved for its music and drumming, dancing, costumes, and colorful Caribbean revelry. It has grown so large that it has been called "the greatest show on earth." Tens of thousands of people participate, and costumes have become so elaborate that it can cost up to $45,000 to outfit a "mas" (masquerade) band.

Folklore, Legends, Stories

The characters featured in Trinidad Carnival celebrations are often based on figures from Caribbean folklore. These include Papa Bois, the king of the forest, and his son, Callaloo, who fights a battle with an evil character called Mancrab.

In 1984, world-famous Trinidadian costume designer Peter Minshall wrote a story featuring Callaloo, called *Callaloo an de Crab*. In the book, Callaloo champions peace among all people when he says, "Callaloo say to put away cutlass. Throw all the ammunition in the sea. And if is love man want, and good life man want to live, is hand have to hold on to hand, is circle have to make, is peace have to put in circle centre, and is prosperity then, and happiness for each and every man."

Other popular figures from island folklore are devils in disguise and the she-devil Diablesse, who is like the sorceress Circe (pronounced SIR-see) in Greek mythology. Diablesse turns men into hogs and causes them to fall over a cliff. Still other characters that are featured are the Douens, or spirits of small children who died before they were baptized. The Douens are mischievous creatures who steal vegetables from people's gardens, and are said to walk with their feet turned backward.

Customs, Traditions, Ceremonies

The main celebration of Carnival begins in Independence Square in the heart of Port-of-Spain, Trinidad, at about 4 A.M., just before dawn, on the Monday before Ash Wednesday. It continues until midnight on Tuesday, with no stopping to sleep, with a final celebration called "las lap."

Smaller parties called fêtes (pronounced FETS) and musical and costume competitions are held for weeks before Carnival, beginning shortly after New Year's Day. People begin planning their costumes for the following year as soon as the current year's Carnival is over. Practice for the steel and calypso band competitions goes on nonstop. Competition is what drives the Carnival celebration in Trinidad—everyone works his or her hardest all year to be the best.

Pre-Carnival weekend festivities

On Saturday night before Carnival, the best steel bands gather for a concert and parade called the Panorama. On Sunday, the Dimanche Gras (pronounced dee-MONSH GRAH; Fat Sunday) activities are held. These include a costume show, a theatrical performance, and the crowning of the Carnival king and queen, as well as the announcement of the singers chosen as calypso monarchs (see "Music, Dance").

J'ouvert

The ceremony that officially opens Carnival in Trinidad is called J'ouvert (pronounced zhoo-VAIR), from the French *jour ouvert,* meaning "opening day." It begins before daybreak, at about 4 A.M., as groups gather in the streets and begin marching toward the center of Port-of-Spain, accompanied by steel drums and calypso bands.

Everyone wears a simple home-made costume for J'ouvert, because smearing one another with mud is a favorite part of the ceremony. J'ouvert is also the time to "jump up," or dance, to the rhythm of the steel drums. Dancing in the streets continues for the next forty-eight hours, until the

A group of Trinidadian and Tobagoan musicians play steel drums on the beach. Carnival has made calypso and steel drum music world famous. Reproduced by permission of Susan D. Rock.

end of Carnival. Another popular pastime during Carnival is just "hanging out" with friends and being "cool"—what Trinidadians call "liming."

Parades and more parades

The J'ouvert, or opening day, parade early in the morning on the Monday before Ash Wednesday is only the first of many Carnival parades in Trinidad. At 9 A.M. on Monday the Ole Mas Parade is held, featuring old-style costumes and folklore characters. Then comes a parade highlighting traditional masks, followed by the military groups. At 2 P.M. the huge Historical and Fantasy Mas Bands Parade is held. At dusk, there is more dancing in the streets with calypso and steel bands.

On Tuesday, everyone is in their finest costumes for the biggest day of Carnival. There is an enormous parade that features masquerade bands and the calypso and steel bands. Huge speakers are mounted on flatbed trucks and posted at intersections. Crowds line the streets and participate in the parades by dancing to the music. Some thirty mas bands, with as many as five thousand costumed members each, parade and dance through the streets.

Each mas band represents a neighborhood or community, and has its own king and queen and star performer.

Las lap.... And that's a wrap!

The final big Carnival celebration before midnight on Tuesday is called "las lap." Everyone gathers at Port-of-Spain's city park, Queen's Park Savannah, for more band competitions, eating, drinking, and dancing. At midnight, Carnival is officially over for another year.

Clothing, Costumes

In Trinidad, work on Carnival costumes goes on all year, with everything coming together after Christmas in a frenzy right up until the night before Carnival. Part of the magic of the costumes is the drama associated with them: each character has a story behind it, often a traditional one, and these dramas are acted out in the streets during the parades. Some character costumes are so ingrained in the country's history that they are featured year after year. Certain individuals become so associated with specific characters that they, too, appear each year.

Groups that wear costumes around a certain theme and dance together in the parades are called masquerade, or "mas," bands. Mas groups wear costumes on any theme they choose; they often portray historical or political themes, including wars and other major events. The groups may have as many as five thousand dancers each.

One of the earliest Carnival costumes in Trinidad was Moko Jumbie, a West African figure who walked on stilts and danced a jig accompanied by a small band composed of flute, drum, and triangle. Other early costumes that were worn by the French and later by freed slaves and other blacks included the garden slave and the Pierrot Grenade (pronounced pyair-ROW greh-NOD), originally a European clown, which evolved into a talkative, richly dressed, strutting, and fearless character who fights with whips or sticks.

The Pierrots wore a decorated, heart-shaped piece of cloth on the front of their costumes, and rival Pierrots would try to flick off the heart of their opponents when they met and fought in the streets.

In about 1900, the Wild Indian costume was introduced. Masqueraders dressed as members of a tribe of native South American Indians called the Guarajo, or Warrahoon, who came in their canoes to trade in Trinidad. Masquerade bands later divided the Wild Indians into the red, blue, black, and white Indians, each with elaborate costumes in those colors.

Later, the Indian costume developed into the Fancy Indian, which resembled the dress of a North American Plains Indian chief, but with much more elaborate headdress and bright, multicolored clothing. The Indian Warrior Band was another group that costumed as American Indians.

Other popular costumes are those of the devil (in French, Diable and shortened to "Jab") and she-devil, or Diablesse; the Midnight Robber; Jammet, who is both male and female; the Burrokeet (or Borokit), a donkey and rider with its own procession; and the clown and bat. Jab Molassi is a vulgar devil who is covered with molasses and smeared with dirt and grease. These evil characters come out during J'ouvert, just before daybreak on the first day of Carnival.

Foods, Recipes

Trinidadians have some favorite dishes that are especially popular at Carnival time. These include salt codfish and a spicy soup made with seafood and a type of large green leaf called callaloo. The soup is served with a flat, pastry-like Indian bread called *roti*.

Salting fish is an old method of preserving fresh fish that was used by Portuguese sailors returning home from codfishing trips to Newfoundland. The fish is slit open, cleaned, and salted. When preparing it later, it is best to soak the fish in water for twenty-four hours, changing the water twice to thoroughly flush out the salt. The fish is then roasted over charcoal. After it cools, the skin and bones are removed, and olive oil and fresh lime juice are sprinkled over it.

Callaloo, also called dasheen or taro, is a root vegetable that is grown in China, Japan, and in the Caribbean. In Trinidad, people love the large, green leaves, which look like elephant ears. They are cooked into a delicious soup along with crab or lobster, salt beef, okra, onions, coconut milk, and spices.

These popular foods are accompanied by a Caribbean favorite—rum punch. Rum punch is made with the alcoholic drink rum and fruit juices. Beer is also popular at Carnival celebrations today.

Arts, Crafts, Games

In Trinidad, Carnival costume design is considered an art and is a very important part of the island's culture. There are workshops, called "mas camps," that are devoted to making Carnival costumes. As many as seventy-five people may work on a single costume.

The king and queen of Carnival wear especially magnificent costumes that are created by well-known costume designers. Some of the costumes can weigh more than one hundred pounds and cost over $5,000. Many are created by native Trinidadian designer Peter Minshall, who has become world famous for his Carnival costumes. Minshall has been designing Carnival costumes since 1974.

In 1983, the king of Carnival wore a papillon (pronounced pah-pee-YON; butterfly) costume designed by Minshall. It had a 25-foot wingspread and was made of fiberglass, fishnet, and more than 200,000 metallic sequins. Designer Wayne Berkeley created a theme in 1982 that included a battleship and war heroes portraying the defeat of Napoleon's forces by the British.

Music, Dance

Trinidad and Tobago is famous for its calypso (pronounced kuh-LIP-soh) and steel drum bands, and for the wild dancing that they accompany during Carnival and other celebrations throughout the year.

Calypso: Voice of the islands

Calypso is a type of song that began with African storytelling. Popular among the slaves in Trinidad and Tobago, it became widespread after slaves were emancipated, or freed, in 1834. Calypso songs were written to make a statement about social or political conditions, to tell stories, or to pass on humorous events that occurred within towns or families. Some were sung to shock the European aristocrats who governed the islands; others were about husbands and wives, or lovers. "Calinda," a chant performed by stick fighters, is one form of singing that was adopted by early calypso bands.

Calypso singers were traditionally accompanied by a string band made up of flute, guitar, cuatro (a four-string guitar), mandolin, banjo, and maracas or shack-shacks (rattles made from hollowed-out gourds filled with seeds). After the 1920s, the trombone, saxophone, clarinet, and cornet were added, which introduced a jazz flavor to the music. While the singer sings the many verses that make up a calypso song, he is joined by about forty band members during the chorus. The audience sings along once they learn the words.

Calypso competitions began when master singers, or "shantwells," composed a song and offered it to be sung by groups all over the island. When one group met another shantwell's group, the two would trade songs and compete by insulting one another, all in fun, to entertain the crowd. In today's calypso "wars," the semifinalists make up funny, insulting songs about their competitors.

Calypso bands practice year-round to compete during Carnival. The week before Carnival begins, they give concerts in halls called "calypso tents." These concerts lead up to the annual competition for "Calypso Monarch," which is held the Sunday before J'ouvert. The title of "monarch" is given to the best band in each musical category, including calypso monarch, soca monarch, and rapso monarch.

The bands not only practice all year, they work on writing original songs. The song chosen as overall best during Carnival competition is called the "Road March." Some of the songs that win honors become international hits. Calypso groups also compete *in Extempo,* which means they compete by making up songs on the spot by pulling topics out of a hat.

Steel bands: Recycling at its most tuneful

When the British banned African drumming at Carnival during the mid-1800s, the former slaves in Trinidad and Tobago created instruments from hollow bamboo poles. They made music by tapping the poles on the ground and hitting them with short sticks. They called the music "tamboo bamboo."

In the 1930s, people used the bamboo sticks to make music by hitting them against empty gin bottles or metal containers. Also around this time, musicians began making music using such metallic items as dustbins, pans, old car gas tanks, and paint cans.

With the discovery and production of oil in Trinidad and Tobago came a creative use of empty fifty-five-gallon oil drums that had been thrown away. In the 1940s, island drummers discovered that these large, metal barrels made wonderful instruments when the tops were cut off and hammered inward to make a pattern of dents that produced different tones. They became the first steel drums, or pans, a new musical instrument created in the twentieth century—and made from recycled materials.

The sound created by organized steel bands won acceptance as a new form of music after a successful concert in London in July 1951. The group invited to perform was called the Trinidad All Stars Percussion Orchestra, or TASPO, and Londoners were amazed at the music they made on their rusty, steel barrel instruments. Steel bands played everything from jazz to classical music, and from that point on the music became a favorite throughout not only the Caribbean and South America, but the world.

The steel drums of today are beautiful, shiny instruments that can be tuned to play notes in four ranges, from high to low, called ping-pong, guitar-pan, cello-pan, and bass. The tones and rhythms bring together the sounds of drums, bamboo, and strings. The music created by steel bands can be enjoyed in open spaces in Trinidad called "panyards," where the bands begin practicing for the public in the weeks before Carnival. During Carnival the bands march through the streets, keeping up a beat that makes everyone want to dance.

Steel band competitions are held a few weeks before Carnival, with some seventy-five bands competing to be one of the twelve groups chosen to play during the official celebration. Large public concerts are given by the semifinalists on the Thursday and Saturday before Carnival. The steel band and calypso performances are part of the excitement that brings thousands of tourists to Port-of-Spain every year for Carnival.

Special Role of Children, Young Adults

Trinidad has a special Children's Carnival, held in Port-of-Spain on the Saturday before Carnival. Children dress in costumes that are every bit as elaborate as those worn by adults, and dance in the Children's Parade. Prizes are given for the best costume. A junior Carnival queen is also crowned on Saturday. Then, on Saturday night, girls carry the flags to welcome the steel band semifinalists chosen in previous competitions as they gather for the big public concert.

For More Information

Ellis, Royston. *Trinidad: Festivals of the World*. Milwaukee, Wis.: Gareth Stevens, 1999.

Urosevich, Patricia. *Trinidad and Tobago*. Philadelphia: Chelsea House, 1998.

Web sites

The Callaloo Company: Peter Minshall. [Online] http://www.callaloo.co.tt (accessed on January 19, 2000).

"Carnival: The Greatest Show on Earth!" [Online] http://www.visittnt.com/ToDo/Events/Carnival (accessed on January 19, 2000).

"Trinidad and Tobago Carnival '99." [Online] http://www.visittnt.com/Carnival1999 (accessed on January 19, 2000).

United States

Name of Holiday: Mardi Gras; Carnival

Introduction

The most well-known Carnival celebrations in the United States are held in the South, where the festivities, especially in Louisiana, are very much French influenced. The name for the largest celebration of Carnival, which is held on the Tuesday before

Lent begins, is Mardi Gras (pronounced MAR-deegrah), French for "Shrove Tuesday" or "Fat Tuesday."

In New Orleans, Louisiana, Carnival officially begins on January 6, Epiphany, with celebrations heating up about two weeks before Mardi Gras. Secret clubs called "krewes" play an important part in organizing masked balls, which begin weeks before Mardi Gras, and huge parades, which start the Friday before Ash Wednesday. Businesses are closed on Lundi Gras (Fat Monday) and Mardi Gras while the whole city takes a vacation to celebrate.

Although the New Orleans Carnival festivities last for weeks and feature traditions that date back hundreds of years, the media tends to focus on the few days that lead up to the Tuesday celebration. It is not surprising, since each year thousands of visitors flock to New Orleans to join in on a modern-day tradition—the nonstop party. During the day, people shop, dance in the streets, and catch trinkets thrown from parade floats. At night, they crowd the avenues of the French Quarter for all-night blowouts that feature drinking, singing, and wild dancing to jazz and rhythm and blues bands.

The oldest Mardi Gras celebration is held in Mobile, Alabama, and features more tame activities, including family-centered parades. Several other cities in the United States, including Galveston, Texas, and Pensacola and Tampa, Florida, also host special Mardi Gras festivities.

History

The celebration of Carnival was brought to the United States by the French, who settled what are now Mobile, Alabama, and New Orleans, Louisiana, in the late 1600s and early 1700s. The first official notice of Mardi Gras occurred on March 3, 1699, when a French explorer established a post on the Mississippi River and called it Pointe de Mardi Gras, after the holiday in France. Mardi Gras was popular under French settlement in New Orleans and Mobile, but when the Spanish took control of the region, they outlawed the celebration.

Carnival festivities in New Orleans were revived in 1827 by a group of students who had just returned from Paris, France, where they had participated in a Mardi Gras celebration. Until 1839, Mardi Gras was celebrated chiefly with balls, but on Fat Tuesday of that year, the first Mardi Gras parade was held—with one float. Mardi Gras as it exists today, with colorful parades, costumes, and many floats, really began in the mid-1800s.

Cowbellions and Mysticks

In 1831, the first U.S. krewes began as a result of an evening of pranks by some young men in Mobile, who were led by Michael Krafft, from Pennsylvania. The boys had been drinking after a New Year's celebration and broke into a hardware store in Mobile, where they stole some cowbells and rakes. They paraded through town, making noise and shouting insults at people. The youths called themselves the Cowbellion de Rakin Society, after the cowbells and rakes they had stolen, and marched in the New Year's Day parade on the following day.

In 1857, six of these young men moved to New Orleans and started a similar society. It later became New Orleans's oldest and most respected krewe, the Mystick

Krewe of Comus. Comus is a god of mirth and spirits featured in the masque (dramatic poem or play) *Comus*, written by English poet John Milton (1608–1674). The Comus Krewe masqueraded as characters from Milton for a Mardi Gras parade and then put on a masked show at a New Orleans opera house, establishing a holiday tradition.

A blending of cultures

Since New Orleans was first founded, immigrants continued to flood to the port city. These included African slaves, Germans, Spaniards, Italians, African Caribbean peoples, and French Canadians, who would later be known as Cajuns. White people of French descent in New Orleans came to be known as Creoles. As all of these cultures mingled, distinct foods and music evolved from a blend of the many different tastes and musical styles. They all influenced parts of Carnival. The black influence on Mardi Gras celebrations grew until, in 1909, the first all-black krewe was formed, called Zulu, after a South African tribe.

Into the present

Early Mardi Gras parades included horses and carriages; later, floats were pulled by mules, which were then replaced by tractors and trucks. During the mid-1800s, Creole maskers in carriages threw flowers and bonbons to women and children on balconies. In the 1870s, some krewes threw candy and peanuts to the crowds and others tossed favors, some costly, to family and friends.

In 1921, the Krewe of Rex started the practice of throwing trinkets to the crowd on a large scale. Photographs of the 1922 parade show everyone in the crowds holding out their arms in hopes of catching the glass beads and necklaces thrown from the floats. By 1960, plastic coins called doubloons had been introduced, and many other throws, such as plastic whistles, soon followed.

During the latter part of the twentieth century, Mardi Gras celebrations became increasingly elaborate, with wealthy citizens spending up to $100,000 on costumes for masked balls and similar amounts spent on parade floats. Today, hundreds of thousands of people flock to New Orleans and other cities for Mardi Gras each year.

Folklore, Legends, Stories

The folklore that contributes to Mardi Gras celebrations in the southern United States originated with the French and other Europeans who settled in the area. Their interest in imitating royalty and aristocracy influenced the crowning of a Mardi Gras king and the costumes of various courts.

The elaborate masked balls and parties held throughout the Mardi Gras season originated with French, Italian, Spanish, and German Carnival celebrations. Added to the European influence was the early krewes' interest in classical literature and mythology, as well as the folklore of the American Indians, the African slaves, and the Caribbean peoples who lived in the southern port cities.

Angels, devils, and mysticks

The early secret clubs organized to plan Mardi Gras activities in Mobile and New Orleans created a U.S. Carnival folklore that was heavily influenced by classic mythology and literature, and the occult. The first New Orleans society, or krewe, was called the Mystick Krewe of Comus.

Revelers dressed as devils take part in a 1999 Carnival celebration. U.S. Carnival folklore has been heavily influenced by classic mythology and literature, and the occult. Reproduced by permission of AP/Wide World Photos.

They not only named their organization after a work written by English poet John Milton, the theme of their first parade was "Demon Actors of 'Paradise Lost.'" *Paradise Lost* is a long poem by Milton that deals with heaven and hell, angels, and Satan. The Comus Krewe's later themes were based on works by ancient Greek and Roman writers, including Homer and Ovid.

This early focus on classical studies and mythology continued to be embraced by later krewes, which adopted names of Greek figures, including Proteus, Hermes, and Apollo, or Greek cities, such as Athens or Corinth. Today the various float, parade, and ball themes are still influenced by the ancient classics.

Customs, Traditions, Ceremonies

New Orleans begins celebrating Carnival on January 6, Epiphany, and continues through Mardi Gras, or Fat Tuesday, the Tuesday before Ash Wednesday. The French-influenced city is known for its formal masked balls, when the wealthy host fancy parties for their friends and associates. Costumes worn at these balls are often traditional ones based on characters from classical literature, mythology, art, or opera. Teenage girls of dating age are introduced to society during many of these balls, which they attend in beautiful costumes.

Mardi Gras, however, is not only for the wealthy. It is a time to drop any class, racial, or other prejudice and simply have fun. People wear whatever costumes strike their fancy and take on secret identities. An unspoken rule in New Orleans during Mardi Gras is "do whatever you like as long as it doesn't harm anyone else."

Secret Carnival societies

An aspect of Carnival in the southern United States that sets it apart from celebrations in other parts of the world are the secretive, members-only Carnival clubs called krewes, or "mystic societies." These are believed to have originated with the French *reynages* (pronounced ray-NAHZH; pretend kingdoms). The reynages consisted of citizens dressed as a king and queen and their court for Carnival celebrations in medieval France.

The oldest society, the Mystick Krewe of Comus, was formed in 1857. The second most respected krewe in New Orleans is the Krewe of Rex, which was formed in 1872 and crowns one of its members official king of Mardi Gras each year. Zulu is another long-standing krewe, formed in 1909, with all African American members.

Today, there are fifty to sixty krewes in New Orleans and some fifty-five in Mobile. They range in number of members from less than one hundred to more than fifteen hundred. Many are open by invitation only to certain members of society; others are open to anyone who can pay the annual dues that cover the costs of the krewe's Mardi Gras activities.

A person may join as many krewes as he or she is invited to and can pay dues for. Because all Mardi Gras parade organizations are completely funded by their members, Mardi Gras has been called "the greatest free show on Earth."

In 1991, the New Orleans City Council introduced a parade organization anti-discrimination ordinance that forbids excluding any person from membership in the secret societies called krewes. In protest of this ordinance, some of the oldest private clubs, including Momus, Comus, and Proteus, no longer parade in the streets. The most recently developed krewes are open and not secretive.

Each krewe that participates has its own float in the Mardi Gras parade. Some of the larger krewes sponsor parades on one of the days preceding Mardi Gras. A few of the newer krewes pay celebrities to ride as guest parade marshals.

Mardi Gras balls and the mystery dance

Mardi Gras in New Orleans officially begins on January 6 with the Bal du Roi (pronounced bahldewRWAH), or King's Ball, a tradition that was brought to America from Paris, France. Round or oval cakes called king's cakes are eaten on this day, and the person finding a toy figure in his cake has to hold the next ball. King's balls are held throughout the Carnival season, with a final ball held on the Tuesday before Ash Wednesday.

Many krewes sponsor their own masked balls, which are usually open to members and guests only, but a few have celebrity entertainers and are open to the public. A king and queen of Mardi Gras and their court reign during the balls, which begin with the staging of a tableau. The tableau consists of krewe members dressed in costume who create a living picture or scene, usually based on a historical, mythological, musical, or narrative theme.

After the tableau, the formal ball begins. In the men's krewes, if a lady has been invited to the ball, she waits until a krewe member gives her name. An invitation given this way is known as a "call-out." Then she gets up and dances with the masked member, who does not reveal his identity. Gentlemen who are not members of the men's krewe but are invited as guests to the ball are called "black coats." They are allowed to dance only after all krewe members have left the dance floor. The women's krewes invite men and issue call-outs for the gentlemen they want to dance with.

Mardi Gras parades

Mardi Gras parades have been held in Mobile and in New Orleans since the early 1800s.

Some scholars say parade floats began as church tableaux that were banished to the streets because they were too outrageous. For many years, the organized krewes have played a big part in these parades, sponsoring floats and riding on them in costume. Other organizations, such as school groups, also enter the parades, with members driving trucks, vans, and decorated vehicles. Parades also include marching bands, dancers, and twirlers.

Dressing in wild costumes and parading is especially popular in the French Quarter of New Orleans. Outside the French Quarter, quieter neighborhoods of New Orleans celebrate with family get-togethers and picnics on the streets and in parks. Smaller towns celebrate with parades as well. Some are boat parades, with floats drifting along on canals, bayous, and rivers. In Mobile, Alabama, Mardi Gras is a legal holiday, as it is in Louisiana, and six parades are held on Fat Tuesday, attended by more than 100,000 people.

Rex, King of Carnival

The king of Carnival in New Orleans is Rex, king of the Krewe of Rex. He is the official king of all Mardi Gras and is also called the King of Tomfools, or the Lord of Misrule. Rex rides on a "throne" parade float in the Fat Tuesday parade. He also receives the keys to the city and rules all day on Mardi Gras.

Throw me somethin', mister!

While it is customary to throw objects during Carnival parades, in New Orleans and Mobile collecting throws is probably the biggest thrill of the season for the general public and for the many tourists who come to Mardi Gras. The tradition of throwing objects during Carnival parades began in the 1830s and became a public nuisance in the 1850s, when people threw dirt, lye, and flour at the crowd. This resulted in a temporary ban on throws.

In the mid-twentieth century, throws became colorful collectibles. As parade floats pass by on Fat Tuesday, costumed krewe members called "maskers" throw hundreds of trinkets into the crowd. These trinkets can be colorful plastic-bead necklaces, aluminum coins called doubloons, plastic cups, stuffed animals, party favors, whistles, plastic har-

Krewe of Rex floats parade through New Orleans, Louisiana, during Mardi Gras in 1993. Rex, king of the Krewe of Rex, is king of Carnival in New Orleans. Reproduced by permission of Archive Photos, Inc.

monicas, toy hand grenades, or just about anything the krewe members decide to give away. The Zulu Krewe once threw hand-painted coconuts to the crowd during Mardi Gras parades.

The crowds lining the streets hold out their arms and chant, "Throw me somethin', mister!" all day long as the beads and other trinkets hit the streets. The trick to successful trinket collecting is to put a foot on any trinket that lands nearby and then reach down to pick it up, so hands do not get trampled.

Most Mardi Gras favors get thrown away eventually, but some of the first doubloons and certain other trinkets have become collector's items. Some throws are saved and used again in later Mardi Gras parades.

Farewell toast to Mardi Gras

In New Orleans, members of the Rex and Comus krewes drink a traditional toast at midnight on Mardi Gras to officially close out the celebration and pronounce the beginning of Lent. The following morning, crowds attend the Ash Wednesday mass at Saint Louis Cathedral.

Clothing, Costumes

Anything goes for Mardi Gras, from formal wear for masked balls to street clothes and painted faces. The krewes often dress in elaborate costumes for their balls and parades. Traditional colors for Mardi Gras are purple, for justice; gold, for power; and green, for faith. These were declared the official Mardi Gras colors in 1872, when members of the Krewe of Rex wore them in their first parade. The bishop who opens the church for Lenten mass on Ash Wednesday wears these colors; they are also used to decorate the king's cakes that are served at king's balls during the Mardi Gras season.

Foods, Recipes

As with Carnival celebrations the world over, Mardi Gras is a time to eat, drink, and be merry to excess before the fasting of Lent. In a region of the United States famous for its cuisine, Louisiana is home to a variety of Carnival feasts.

Cajun and Creole

Traditional foods of southern Louisiana came from a combination of recipes brought by French Canadian, African, German, Spanish, and Caribbean immigrants, with some American Indian traditions included.

The French Canadians came from a part of Nova Scotia called Acadia. Their name was eventually shortened from Acadians to Cajuns. This name was given to the blend of recipes making up the spicy Louisiana Cajun cooking that includes dishes such as jambalaya, a blend of rice, seafood, sausage, chicken, or other meat, and spices; gumbo, a spicy thick stew of seafood, chicken, sausage, or other meat, and onions, peppers, celery, and okra; and blackened redfish.

Louisiana Creoles are white people of aristocratic French and other European descent. Creole cooking developed primarily in New Orleans, with input from not only French settlers but also Spanish, African, American Indian, and Italian communities.

Spanish influence included the addition of tomatoes and peppers to a thick French soup stock. Germans brought sausages and cheeses; Italians contributed garlic, bread crumbs, and red gravies; islanders from the West Indies introduced tropical vegetables and a slow-cooking method called braising. African American farmers influenced Creole cooking by adding vegetables like okra, yams, onions and garlic, and herbs.

Creole cooking uses many of the same ingredients as Cajun cooking, including fresh vegetables, seafood, and rice, but uses more fats, such as butter and cream. Some Creole dishes are crawfish etouffé, which is stewed crawfish; shrimp Creole, a spicy shrimp stew with garlic, onions, peppers, and celery in a tomato base, served over rice; and for dessert, bananas Foster, bananas sauteed in a sauce of butter, sugar, cinnamon, and rum and served over vanilla ice cream.

In addition to Cajun and Creole food, family and friends sharing Mardi Gras festivities might prepare typically American fare, including pork or beef ribs, hot dogs, hamburgers, or steaks.

Fried delights

As in most other parts of the world where Carnival is celebrated, a fried doughnut-like pastry is popular. In New Orleans it is the French *beignet* (pronounced bane-YAY), a square fritter. Other regions of the United States borrow traditions from a variety of cultures. For instance, the Polish pastry called paczki (pronounced POONCH-key) is a jelly-filled doughnut that has become popular across the United States.

Fit for a king

The food most closely associated with Mardi Gras is the king's cake, a round or oval cake eaten on Three Kings Day, January 6, and throughout the Carnival season at king's balls. These cakes are striped with frosting in purple, green, and gold, the symbolic colors of Mardi Gras. A tiny figure is hidden inside each cake; the person who finds the figure in his cake must buy the next cake or host the next king's ball.

The craftsmen that specialize in designing and making Mardi Gras parade floats are considered true artists. Reproduced by permission of AP/Wide World Photos.

Arts, Crafts, Games

The craftsmen that specialize in designing and making Mardi Gras parade floats are considered true artists. Floats can range from the small, formal, and delicate floats of the Comus Krewe, which are made with a lot of paper sculpture and gold and silver foil, to large representations of people or animals, like the Rex Krewe's huge fattened ox float.

Music, Dance

The same ethnic groups that stirred their foods and recipes together in a melt-

Making a Miniature Mardi Gras Float

To make a miniature Mardi Gras float you will need the following items: a shoebox; green, or other colored, tissue paper or foil; tape; a clown, king, princess, or other character doll; play coins; Mardi Gras beads; glitter; sequins; stick-on plastic jewels; jelly beans or hard candies; ribbons; artificial flowers.

Remove lid from the shoebox and turn the box over so the bottom side is up. Stand the lid on end and attach it to one end of the box to make a "float" with a back. Cover the bottom and lid of the box with colored tissue paper or foil. Decorate the float along a theme such as an ocean kingdom or an enchanted garden. Be creative, using items you have on hand. Dress the character dolls as king and queen of Mardi Gras, and place on top of the float. Make several floats and stage a Mardi Gras parade.

ing pot on the American Gulf Coast also mingled their music and dance. New Orleans is famous for its jazz, and the French Quarter is probably the best place to hear some of the world's best jazz musicians, during Mardi Gras or at any other time of year. Rhythm and blues is another southern musical tradition.

Both jazz and rhythm and blues are influenced by the black folk music of the American South and have a character-istic rhythm called syncopation. Jazz bands are typically made up of such instruments as guitar, drums, horns, saxophone, and piano, and play tunes with faster rhythms. Rhythm and blues, like blues music, is often sad, soulful music, played using guitar, bass guitar, drums, harmonica, and perhaps piano. Rhythm and blues has a stronger and faster beat than blues, however.

A few of the songs that have been made famous during Mardi Gras over the years are: "Go To the Mardi Gras," "Carnival Time," "Street Parade," "Handa Wanda," "Mardi Gras Mambo," "Iko Iko," "They All Ask for You," "Wade in the River," and "If Ever I Cease to Love."

A song for royalty

In 1872, Alexis Romanov, a Russian grand duke, was making a tour of the United States. During his travels, he reputedly fell madly in love with Lydia Thompson, an American actress and star, who was known for the song "If Ever I Cease to Love." He was so infatuated with the actress that he followed her to New Orleans. The duke's visit coincided with the beginning of Mardi Gras, and once the krewes found out that real royalty was in town, they began to make preparations to give him a royal welcome.

The Rex Krewe anointed one of their members as king of Mardi Gras, and they took over city hall for the day. Duke Alexis was provided a throne and he was serenaded, almost nonstop, to the tune of "If Ever I Cease to Love." The song has remained an integral part of Mardi Gras to this day.

Special Role of Children, Young Adults

Even though children do not participate in the adult rowdiness of the New Orleans French Quarter during Carnival, they do enjoy attending the Mardi Gras parades held elsewhere in the city. Families often make a day of it, and enjoy picnic lunches before the parades begin. As a special treat for children, each school in New Orleans holds its own parade and pageant.

Mobile's Mardi Gras is geared toward participation by the whole family and includes picnics, block parties, barbeques, boat parades, children's parades, and marching bands.

For More Information

Kinser, Samuel. *Carnival American Style: Mardi Gras at New Orleans and Mobile.* Chicago: University of Chicago Press, 1990.

MacMillan, Diane. *Mardi Gras.* Enslow Publishers, 1997.

Schindler, Henri. *Mardi Gras: New Orleans.* New York: Abbeville Press, 1997.

Web sites

"Carnival New Orleans." [Online] http://www.carnivalneworleans.com (accessed on January 20, 2000).

"Mardi Gras New Orleans." [Online] http://www.MardiGrasNewOrleans.com (accessed on January 20, 2000).

"Mardi Gras 2000: Information Source for the Gras." [Online] http://www.mardigrasday.com (accessed on January 20, 2000).

Carnival Sources

Clynes, Tom. *Wild Planet!* Detroit, Mich.: Visible Ink, 1995, pp. 40–43, 61–63, 464–69, 521–24.

Dineen, Jacqueline. *Feasts and Festivals.* Philadelphia: Chelsea House, 1999, p. 32.

Field, Carol. *Celebrating Italy.* New York: William Morrow, 1990, pp. 343–52, 369–72.

Gall, Timothy L., ed. *Worldmark Encyclopedia of Cultures and Daily Life.* Vol. 2—Americas. Detroit, Mich.: Gale, 1998, pp. 15, 88–90, 423–25.

Greenberg, Harriet, and Arnold Greenberg. *Rio Alive.* New York: Alive Publications, 1988, pp. 17–18, 46–47, 167–72.

Griffin, Robert H., and Ann H. Shurgin, eds. *The Folklore of World Holidays.* 2nd ed. Farmington Hills, Mich.: Gale, 1999, pp. 132–50.

Guillermoprieto, Alma. *Samba.* New York: Alfred A. Knopf, 1990, pp. 25–26, 37, 211–15.

MacKie, Cristine. *Life and Food in the Caribbean.* New York: New Amsterdam, 1991, pp. 103, 115–16.

Santino, Jack. *All Around the Year: Holidays and Celebrations in American Life.* Chicago: University of Illinois Press, 1994, pp. 88–96.

Siefker, Phyllis. *Santa Claus, Last of the Wild Men.* Jefferson, N.C.: McFarland, 1997, pp. 124–25, 135, 138–41.

Teixeira, Sergio Alves. "Samba Time!" *UNESCO Courier,* December 1989, pp. 38–41.

Thompson, Sue Ellen, ed. *Holiday Symbols 1998.* Detroit, Mich.: Omnigraphics, 1998, pp. 51–54.

Williams, A. R. "The Wild Mix of Trinidad and Tobago." *National Geographic,* March 1994, pp. 66, 86–87.

Web sites

Brophy, James M. "Mirth and Subversion: Carnival in Cologne." *History Today,* July 1, 1997. [Online] http://www.elibrary.com/s/edumark (accessed on January 23, 2000).

"Carnival Around the World." [Online] http://www.festivals.com/carnival (accessed on January 13, 2000).

"Carnival Time in Italy." [Online] http://www.notti.italiane.com/carnevaleb.html (accessed on February 9, 2000).

Cowin, Andrew. "Fat Tuesday's Rollin' 'Round Germany." *Newsday,* January 23, 1994. [Online] http://www.elibrary.com/s/edumark (accessed on February 17, 2000).

Rilette, Christy. "The History of Creole Cuisine." [Online] http://www.scils.rutgers.edu/~crilette/creolehistory.html (accessed on February 9, 2000).

Thomasson, Emma. "German Women Take Over for Carnival." *Reuters,* February 6, 1997. [Online] http://www.elibrary.com/s/edumark (accessed on March 17, 1999).

Christmas

Also Known As:
Genna or Gannā (Ethiopia)
Il Natale (Italy)
Pasko Ng Bata, Christmas, or Navidad (Philippines)
Jul (Sweden)
Christmas, Yule, Noel or
Feast of the Nativity (United States)
Navidad (Venezuela)

Introduction

Christmas is a time of year when Christians throughout the world join together to celebrate the birth of Jesus Christ (c. 6 B.C.–c. A.D. 30), the founder of Christianity. Originally called the Feast of the Nativity, Christmas is nearly two thousand years old. The rituals and celebrations associated with Christmas are a combination of Christian religious practices and customs that were introduced by people of different cultures throughout the world.

In Western churches, Christmas Eve is celebrated on December 24 and Christmas Day on December 25, dates chosen in Rome in 336. There is no written record of the actual date of Christ's birth, however, and Eastern Orthodox churches celebrate Christmas according to the Julian calendar on January 7.

The Eastern Orthodox Church is a Christian community that split with the Roman Catholic Church. The split started with countries in eastern Europe and western Asia. Today there are Eastern Orthodox communities in countries all over the world, including the United States. The Julian calendar is thirteen days behind the Gregorian calendar, which was first introduced in the 1500s and continues to be used today by most countries.

Advent and Epiphany are other Christian holidays associated with Christmas. Advent is a four-week period of preparation for the coming of Christmas, and Epiphany marks the end of the Christmas season. Epiphany is celebrated in many countries as the day on which the Three Wise Men, or Three Kings, visited the infant Jesus in Bethlehem, taking him gifts of gold, frankincense, and myrrh. The Eastern Orthodox Church celebrates Epiphany as the day of Jesus' baptism by John the Baptist.

History

Christians began to celebrate the birth of Jesus Christ on December 25, in about A.D. 336 in Rome, Italy, during the rule of Emperor Constantine the Great (ruled 306–37). They called this festival the Feast of the Nativity. Nativity celebrations were similar to early non-Christian Roman festivals, and featured much feasting, drinking, and merrymaking.

Holiday Fact Box: Christmas

Themes

Celebrating the Nativity, the birth of Jesus Christ; gift giving; trimming and lighting Christmas trees; decorating homes and cities; feasting and merrymaking; singing carols; spreading goodwill and charity.

Type of Holiday

Christmas is a major religious holiday during which Christians the world over celebrate the birth of Jesus Christ, who is the founder of Christianity. Christmas also has many secular (nonreligious) traditions observed by Christians and non-Christians alike.

When Celebrated

Although the Bible, the sacred book of Christianity, does not include a specific date for the birth of Jesus Christ, Christmas Eve is celebrated each year on December 24 and Christmas Day on December 25. The Eastern Orthodox Church, which still follows the Julian calendar, celebrates Christmas on January 7. In Roman Catholic and Episcopal churches, the Christmas season begins with Advent. Advent is a time of preparation held during the four weeks before Christmas. January 6, or Epiphany, is a religious holiday marking the official ending of the Christmas season. The "twelve days of Christmas" referred to in the song by the same name are the days that fall between Christmas Day and Epiphany.

By the end of the fourth century, Christianity had become the official religion of the Roman Empire and, by 432, the celebration of the Nativity extended to the Eastern Church in Constantinople (now Istanbul, Turkey) and then to Egypt. As Christianity spread, so too did the tradition of celebrating the birth of Jesus on December 25. The date was established in England by the end of the sixth century; in Scandinavia (the region in northern Europe composed of Denmark, Norway, Sweden, and Finland) about two hundred years later; and throughout Europe by the thirteenth century. It eventually became the most important Christian religious festival of the year.

In the late ninth century, King Alfred of England (ruled 871–99) extended the Nativity celebration from December 25 to Epiphany, on January 6. In about 1050, the Feast of the Nativity became known in Europe as Cristes mæsse, Old English for "mass of Christ."

Feasting and making merry

During the Middle Ages (about 500–1500), Christmas was Christianity's most popular festival, although it was more like the modern Carnival than like Christmas today. In England and other parts of Europe, people crowned a Bishop of Fools, or a Lord of Misrule, who reigned over a Feast of Fools.

After church services on Christmas, many people celebrated by drinking, feasting, dancing, and parading in costumes. These Europeans also held on to many customs of their old winter solstice celebrations, such as decorating with greenery, exchanging gifts, burning a huge log in the fireplace, and lighting candles.

British kings and queens spent small fortunes on elaborate Christmas dinners and pageants. But as economic times grew hard during the late sixteenth and early seventeenth centuries, the focus of Christmas changed to one of charity toward the poor, and the more wealthy families treated their servants to the best food and drink in the household during the Christmas season.

The spread of Christianity

In the 1500s, Spanish and Portuguese missionaries introduced Catholicism to the Indians of Mexico and much of Central and South America. Spanish Roman Catholic missionaries also introduced Christianity to the native islanders of the Philippines, beginning in the mid-1500s. Today, Christianity is the major religion in the Philippines, making it the only Asian country that is predominantly Christian.

Both the native Indians of Mexico and Central and South America and the Filipino natives were attracted to the drama and ceremony of the Catholic Church, especially during holiday celebrations. Over time, the religious meaning of the holiday has remained the most important focus of Christmas celebrations in these countries.

Ethiopian Christians have been part of the Coptic Christian Church since neighboring Egyptian Coptics introduced this faith to Ethiopia during the fourth century. They celebrate Christmas on January 7, according to the Julian calendar, still followed in the Eastern Orthodox Church. Their Christmas is very much a religious celebration and is much less commercial

Thousands of little Christmas lights glow in front of Saint Peter's Cathedral in Zurich, Switzerland, in 1997. Reproduced by permission of AP/Wide World Photos.

than in other countries. British, French, Dutch, and other European colonists introduced Christmas to many other parts of Africa, and their Western customs often melded with African traditions to form a unique celebration.

Christmas is banned

During the sixteenth century in Europe, a reformation took place in the Roman Catholic Church. People who objected to some of the Catholic rituals split from the Church and formed a new branch of Christianity known as Protestantism. Members of a strict group of Protestants, called the Puritans, took control of the government in England. As part of the reform, the English soldier and statesman Oliver Cromwell (1599–1658), a Puritan leader, tried to put a stop to the observance of Christmas.

From 1642 to 1656, Cromwell and the Puritan Commonwealth made laws against Christmas practices such as plays, feasting, decorating, and preaching about the birth of Christ. During this time, many people celebrated secretly in their homes, giving up the big public displays and festivities. When the monarchy was restored in 1660, holidays were once again celebrated openly. Christmas still had more secular customs than religious ones, but the celebrations were not as elaborate as they once had been.

Puritans who immigrated to the New England colonies in America during the early to middle 1600s did not believe that holidays should be celebrated. In 1659, the General Courts of Massachusetts and Connecticut outlawed Christmas, and soon nearly all of New England did the same. Settlers in Virginia continued to celebrate Christmas, however, and colonists along the Atlantic coast had mixed feelings about the holiday. By 1681, the law against Christmas was abolished, but some New England states still did not celebrate Christmas, even as late as 1810.

A Christmas revival

In the 1700s, Dutch, German, and Irish immigrants began settling in what are now New York, Pennsylvania, and the mid-Atlantic states. They introduced to America such Christmas customs as decorating a Christmas tree, hanging up Christmas stockings, and telling children legends about a gift bearer, who would later develop into Santa Claus.

The celebration of Christmas grew and flourished, and by the late 1800s Christmas had become the year's most popular holiday. By 1890, every state and territory had declared Christmas a legal holiday. Churches embraced the Christmas celebration around the beginning of the twentieth century, when the first Sunday Schools organized Christmas programs for children to perform.

Modern Christmas: Glitter and faith

With an emphasis on gift giving, decorating, and feasting, Christmas became increasingly commercialized from the 1800s on. During the late 1800s, department stores in the United States began using live "Santas" and Santa art in advertisements to sell toys and other gifts at Christmastime.

Christian missionaries to many Asian and African countries introduced Christmas customs along with the teachings of Christianity. As communication and travel became more advanced, the Christmas customs of the Western world made their way to countries everywhere. Many Christmas customs, such as giving gifts, decorating a tree, displaying a Nativity scene or a Santa Claus figure, and decorating with lights, have filtered into countries such as China, Japan, and India, where only a small percentage of the population is Christian.

China now manufactures many of the world's Christmas decorations, and many Asians decorate their own cities at Christmas much like those in the West, even though they do not observe the religious aspects of the holiday.

Folklore, Legends, Stories

For Christians, the story at the center of the Christmas holiday is the story of the birth of Jesus Christ. This story is told and retold every year and is embraced by Christians in every culture. Many of the customs and traditions still celebrated have elements that originally came from that night in Bethlehem so long ago.

The Christmas story

Although historians are uncertain about the exact date and particulars surrounding the birth of Jesus, the story of his birth is recounted several times in the Bible, which is the sacred book of Christianity. According to the version found in Luke 2:7–11, Jesus was born two thousand years ago to a woman named Mary. Mary gave birth in a stable located in the city of Bethlehem, near Jerusalem in present-day Israel:

> And she brought forth her first-born son, and wrapped him in swaddling clothes, and laid him in a manger; because there was no room for them in the inn. And there were in the same country shepherds abiding in the field, keeping watch over their flocks by night. And, lo, the angel of the Lord came upon them, and the glory of the Lord shone round about them: and they were sore afraid. And the angel said unto them, "Fear not: for, behold, I bring you good tidings of great joy, which shall be to all people. For unto you is born this day, in the city of David, a Savior, which is Christ the Lord."

Classic Christmas literature

Hundreds of stories and poems have been written about Christmas, especially during the nineteenth and twentieth centuries as Christmas blossomed. One of them is *The Fir Tree,* written by Danish author Hans Christian Andersen (1805–1875). It is the story of a young evergreen whose greatest hour comes when it is decorated and becomes a wealthy family's Christmas tree.

American author Washington Irving (1783–1859) is credited with reviving Christmas celebrations in the United States and contributing to the Santa Claus legend with his *Knickerbocker's History of New York,* published on Saint Nicholas Day in 1809. In 1822, Clement Clarke Moore, an American professor, further established the Santa Claus myth when he wrote a poem called "A Visit from St. Nicholas" for his children. Also known as "'Twas the Night Before Christmas," it soon became one of the most popular poems in America's history and is still read by millions on Christmas Eve.

Dickens's *A Christmas Carol*

A fictional story that has become a Christmas classic is *A Christmas Carol,* written by English author Charles Dickens (1812–1870). The story was written in 1843, and has helped popularize such Christmas traditions as giving gifts; decorating with holly, evergreens, and mistletoe; serving the Christmas feast; and spreading goodwill and charity toward the poor at Christmas.

The main character in *A Christmas Carol* is Ebenezer Scrooge, a bitter man who has little to say about Christmas except "Bah! Humbug!" The character was so well written, and his story told so often, that the term "scrooge" is now used to describe any individual who is mean-spirited and stingy. On Christmas Eve, Scrooge is visited by three ghosts: the ghost of Christmas Past, the

Gerald Dickens, the great-great-grandson of Charles Dickens, acts with a child from the audience during a 1999 performance of the elder Dickens's *A Christmas Carol*. Reproduced by permission of AP/Wide World Photos.

ghost of Christmas Present, and the ghost of Christmas Future. Through them, Scrooge sees his past mistakes, the state of his life in the present, and a glimpse of his lonely future if he does not have a change of heart. Scrooge sees the light and the story ends in a flurry of happiness and good cheer.

Customs, Traditions, Ceremonies

Over time, every country, every culture, and even every family that celebrates Christmas has developed unique customs and traditions. Some of the traditions date back thousands of years, others have been adapted much more recently, but all share the common elements of peace, kindness, joy, and hope. Attending church services is a common way to celebrate the holiday in Christian communities. Other traditions that have both religious and nonreligious roots include decorating with greenery, gift giving, sending Christmas cards, hanging stockings by the chimney, and feasting.

Christmas countdown: Advent traditions

Since the ninth century, Christians throughout the world have celebrated

Advent, which begins on the Sunday nearest November 30 and lasts until midnight on Christmas Eve. The word "advent" means "coming," and this period of several weeks is a time to prepare for the celebration of Jesus' birth. People who attend Advent church services prepare for the celebration of Jesus' birth by praying and reflecting. Advent is also a time for baking, cleaning, shopping, decorating, and making gifts.

Advent is observed in most Christian churches, including Catholic, Lutheran, Anglican, and Episcopal. The first Sunday of Advent is also considered by most to begin the official church year. Traditional ways of observing Advent in individual homes are through the Advent calendar, the Advent wreath, and the burning of Advent candles. These customs began in Germany and in Scandinavia.

The Advent calendar is a large Christmas picture—sometimes a house with many windows—on heavy cardboard, with smaller pictures for each day of the Advent season. Each small picture is covered by a flap with the date printed on it. One flap is lifted each day to uncover a picture, a Bible verse, and perhaps a small treat. The largest picture is a Nativity scene for Christmas Eve, the last day of Advent.

An Advent wreath is a flat wreath, usually placed on a table, that is made of holly or evergreens. Nestled inside the greenery are four candles—one for each Sunday of Advent. One candle is lit on the evening of the first Sunday, two on the second, and so forth. A large red candle is often added to the Advent wreath on Christmas Day to represent Jesus Christ. In Germany, a different version of the Advent wreath is the Star of Seven, a candlestick with seven branches. The candles are lit in a special pattern for each Sunday of Advent.

An Advent candle has the days of Advent printed on its side. It is lit every evening and allowed to burn until the candle burns down to the next date. By the time Christmas arrives, the candle has burned completely.

Decorating with Christmas greenery

Decorating with holly, evergreen branches, fragrant herbs, laurel, ivy, moss, and mistletoe was a holiday tradition long before Christmas celebrations began. Because they remained green throughout the winter season, these plants were considered a symbol of hope for returning life and were often brought indoors to freshen stale winter air and brighten up rooms.

The early Romans decorated with laurel, evergreens, and flowers and made laurel crowns for heroes in battle. In both Rome and Scandinavia, enemies who met under mistletoe in the forest would put down their weapons and make peace. For centuries, mistletoe has kept its meaning as a symbol of peace and love.

It is a modern tradition that when a girl stands under the mistletoe, usually hung in a doorway or from a ceiling during the Christmas season, she can be kissed. According to an old custom, a boy should give a girl one of the mistletoe's white berries for every kiss. When the berries are all gone, there are no kisses left.

To the early Christians, holly was a sacred plant. Its sharp-pointed leaves and red berries symbolized the crown of thorns that Jesus wore when he was nailed to the

Poinsettias decorate the entrance to the National Cathedral in Washington, D.C., during Christmastime 1996. Several legends tell of the plant's origin. Reproduced by permission of AP/Wide World Photos.

cross in the biblical story of his death. Holly is sometimes called Christ-thorn. The prickly leaves represent the thorns, and the holly's red berries are like the drops of blood Jesus shed when the thorns pierced his skin. The holly wreath that is so popular today as a Christmas decoration also resembles the crown of thorns.

The poinsettia, with its bright red upper leaves that resemble a flower, is known as the Flower of the Holy Night in Mexico and Central America, its native

land. Joel R. Poinsett, of South Carolina, brought the plant to North America in 1828, and it has become a favorite decorative plant at Christmas. Several legends tell of its origin in Mexico. One is about a poor child who had no gift to place before the Christmas Nativity scene at church and knelt in the snow to pray. A poinsettia sprang up through the snow, and the boy presented it as his gift to the Christ child.

Giving and receiving gifts

The first account of gift giving is found in the biblical story of the Three Wise Men, or Three Kings, who brought gifts of gold, frankincense, and myrrh to the infant Jesus (Matthew 2:1–11). The custom of gift giving is also closely associated with Saint Nicholas of Myra, the fourth-century bishop known for his boundless kindness and generosity.

In the United States, German immigrants to America began giving Christmas gifts during the middle 1700s, and Dutch immigrants gave gifts at the New Year. Most of the early gifts were simple: clothing, handkerchiefs or scarves, and fruit. In the early South, plantation owners gave slaves the day off, and some also gave them money or clothing in a Christmas box, following the English custom of Boxing Day, when people gave gifts to servants and public workers.

By the 1850s, merchants had realized they could make a good profit from holiday gift giving, and people were out shopping by the thousands during the weeks before Christmas. Today, according to one study, about 97 percent of Americans buy Christmas presents for family and friends, and approximately $60 billion is spent on Christmas each year in the United

Boxing Day

Boxing Day, December 26, is celebrated in the United Kingdom, Canada, Australia, New Zealand, and the Bahamas. It began during the Middle Ages, about one thousand years ago, when priests would open the church "alms boxes" (boxes used to collect money for the poor) on Saint Stephen's Day and distribute the money to those in need.

Boxing Day evolved into a time for giving gifts to servants and apprentices, and to public workers such as policemen, mailmen, trash collectors, deliverymen, porters, and errand boys. Sometimes these workers brought wooden boxes around to homes, and family members dropped money into them. Other families delivered boxes filled with useful items like clothes, food, and boots.

Today, people usually give money, as a tip, to these workers. Boxing Day is a legal holiday; most stores remained closed on this day until about 1970. Now stores are open, and many people wait until Boxing Day to do their shopping, because everything goes on sale. It is also an extra day to spend with family and friends after Christmas Day.

States alone. People in many other countries throughout the world do the same thing, but usually on a smaller scale.

In Thailand, department stores run gift sales and wrap purchases, and hotel employees dress up as Santa's elves. Santa Claus is also a familiar sight in Buddhist Japan, where he is associated with look-alike American figure Colonel Sanders of Kentucky Fried Chicken restaurants. On Christmas Eve, young Japanese men take their dates to an expensive dinner and buy them expensive jewelry.

In the Philippines, people donate wrapped gifts to poor children, and Santa Claus makes appearances in the streets and stores throughout the season. The Three Wise Men, who also visit department stores, give gifts to Filipino children on Epiphany. Children leave straw out on the eve of Epiphany for the "royal camels." After mass on Christmas Day and on Epiphany, parents take their children to visit their elders and exchange gifts with them.

The commercialization of Christmas has not reached Ethiopia and some other parts of Africa to the degree it has most other countries. Some churches do, however, put up Christmas trees and children are given small presents. In many other parts of Africa, stores stock a large supply of dolls, games, and toys at Christmastime.

Sending Christmas cards

The first true Christmas card was produced in 1843 in England by an artist named John Callcott Horsley at the request of Sir Henry Cole, founder of the Victoria and Albert Museum in London. The hand-colored card read, "A Merry Christmas and a Happy New Year to You."

The art of Christmas card design: In the early 1850s, R. H. Pease, an engraver from Albany, New York, made the first Christmas card in the United States. German-born printer Louis Prang, of Boston, created the first commercially successful Christmas cards, beginning in 1875. Prang wanted his cards to be more than Christmas greetings; he saw them as small, affordable works of art. His first attempts were more like Valentine's Day cards, designed with colorful flowers and birds, but Prang's artists soon began producing winter scenes featuring children, Santa, and toys, with borders of holly, ivy, and mistletoe. The most expensive cards had silk fringe around the edges and cost about one dollar.

A growing new tradition: During the 1900s, Christmas cards continued to grow in popularity in both Europe and the United States. The most expensive cards were trimmed with silk, satin, lace, tinsel, or feathers and were perfumed. Some had pop-up or fold-out pictures and could be given as Christmas gifts. The practice also caught on in Latin America, Australia, and some parts of Africa. Cards produced in countries in the Southern Hemisphere usually reflect the summertime atmosphere of Christmas and do not include such familiar subjects as snowmen and holly.

As mail delivery became faster, more reliable, and less expensive, more cards were sent. By the mid-1950s, a billion and a half Christmas cards were being mailed in the United States each year. That figure doubled by the 1970s. Sending cards for Hanukkah or Kwanzaa, which are both celebrated around the same time of year as Christmas, also became popular in the 1980s and 1990s. Today, a growing trend is to design cards on the computer and send them via the Internet.

Stockings ... hung by the chimney with care

The origin of the custom of hanging up a stocking to receive small gifts on Christmas Eve is uncertain. Some say it began with the real Saint Nicholas of Myra, who lived during the fourth century. Legends say that he threw three bags of gold into the windows of three poor sisters in Italy so they would each have a dowry and could marry. According to one version of the legend, the bags of money were shaped like stockings; another version claims he dropped the bags down the chimney and they landed in stockings hanging by the fire to dry.

Dutch children once put their shoes on the hearth on December 5, Saint Nicholas Eve, in hopes that he would come and fill them with sweets and presents. During the 1600s, Dutch immigrants introduced the custom to New York, then called New Amsterdam. In the United States, however, shoes were eventually replaced with stockings, which were hung on Christmas Eve instead of Saint Nicholas Eve. In some countries, children still place their shoes out for Santa, or one of his counterparts.

After the 1823 publication of Clement C. Moore's poem "A Visit from St. Nicholas," in which "the stockings were hung by the chimney with care in hopes that Saint Nicholas soon would be there,"

The Christmas Seals Campaign

At the turn of the twentieth century, tuberculosis was a deadly and widespread disease. It was so rampant that there were not enough hospitals for those who needed treatment. In 1903, a Danish postal clerk, Einar Holboell, had an idea for raising money to help those with the disease—selling a special Christmas stamp for cards and letters and giving the profits to the National Tuberculosis Association of Denmark. By 1904, his idea had become a reality. More than four million stamps were sold the first year, raising about $18,000. The Christmas stamp was soon adopted in Sweden and Norway.

In the United States, a well-known journalist and social worker, Jacob Riis, who was born in Denmark and had lost six brothers to tuberculosis, wrote an article about the success of the Christmas stamp in his native country. Emily Bissell, who worked with the Delaware Red Cross, read the article and thought it was a wonderful idea. Her cousin Joseph Wales, a doctor at a poorly funded tuberculosis hospital, had asked her for help in raising money to improve the shabby center.

Emily drew a design for a special Christmas seal—a red cross in the center of a half-wreath of holly—hoping it would be as successful as the Scandinavian stamp. The seals were offered for sale at the Wilmington, Delaware, post office in December 1907. But it took a lot of work and help from a Philadelphia newspaper editor, the chief justice of the U.S. Supreme Court, and U.S. President Theodore Roosevelt (1858–1919) before the Christmas Seals campaign began to be successful. Supported by the Red Cross in 1908, the campaign began raising thousands and then millions of dollars each year for the fight against tuberculosis. Researchers developed successful treatments for the disease, and the number of cases was greatly reduced.

Today, the American Lung Association uses Christmas Seals to raise money for the prevention of tuberculosis and other lung diseases, including asthma. The Christmas Seal emblem is the double-barred cross, adopted in 1919 because of its association with the leader of the first religious Crusade, Godfrey of Lorraine. New art is created each year for the Christmas Seals; the first seals are now valuable collector's items.

hanging Christmas stockings became an established American custom. Today, many children decorate Christmas stockings and hang them on Christmas Eve. In the morning, so the tradition goes, children who have been good throughout the year find candy, money, and little gifts. Those who have been naughty find a lump of coal or a switch used for spanking in their stockings.

Epiphany, or the Twelfth Day of Christmas

Christians began celebrating the Feast of the Epiphany around the beginning of the third century, even before they began to celebrate Christmas. Epiphany, which means "manifestation," originally commemorated three events in the life of Christ: his birth; the visit by the Three Wise Men; and his baptism, which is a Christian ceremony using water to cleanse an individual and admit him into the Christian faith.

In western Europe, Scandinavia, North and South America, and parts of Asia, Epiphany—celebrated on January 6—represents the day on which the Three Wise Men, or the Three Kings, brought gifts of gold, frankincense, and myrrh to the baby Jesus in Bethlehem (Holy Bible, Matthew 2:1–11). In Eastern Orthodox churches, Epiphany is celebrated as the day of Jesus' baptism by John the Baptist in the river Jordan.

The evening before Epiphany is also called Twelfth Night, and has traditionally been a night for fun and games. Special foods are served, like the French *galette des rois* (pronounced guh-LET duh RWAH; cake of the kings), a round pastry with almond filling and a charm hidden inside. In Italy, La Befana, a Christmas witch who gives children toys, similar to Santa Claus, delivers her gifts on Epiphany Eve.

The traditional Christmas carol "The Twelve Days of Christmas," which probably dates back to the 1500s, tells how wealthy people gave one another gifts on each of the twelve days of Christmas—from Christmas Day through Epiphany. In many homes with Nativity scenes on display, the figures of the Three Wise Men are moved closer to the manger each day after Christmas, and on Epiphany they are placed near the infant Jesus figure.

Epiphany marks the end of the Christmas season and is a day for taking down Christmas decorations. Some towns hold parades in which children dress as the Three Wise Men. An important ceremony performed in many countries at Epiphany is the Blessing of the Waters, in which a priest blesses the baptismal waters of the church and then blesses a river, lake, or the sea by throwing or lowering a cross into the water. Divers sometimes compete to be the first to retrieve the cross and receive gifts from townspeople.

Clothing, Costumes

People dress their best to go to midnight mass or to Christmas Day church services and to attend Christmas parties, plays, and concerts. Red and green are considered Christmas colors in many parts of the world, so a Christmas outfit may include these colors, in combination with white or black, or gold or silver.

In North America, Europe, and northern Asia, Christmas comes at midwinter, so people wear their warmest sweaters, boots, and coats. South of the equator, Christmas comes at midsummer. In South America, Africa, southern Asia, Australia, and New Zealand, people dress in lightweight summer clothing and might spend Christmas Day at the beach having a cookout rather than building a snowman or roasting chestnuts by the fire.

Costumes: From simple to spectacular

One of the most popular Christmas costumes is Santa Claus, but the red and white of Santa's suit were originally the colors of the bishop's robes worn by Saint Nicholas of Myra during the fourth century. Modern-day church officials also wear these colors, stitched into beautifully decorated red, gold, and white vestments, or robes, for Christmas services.

Costumes for Christmas pageants include everything from the simple robes of the Holy Family (Mary, Joseph, and the Christ child) and shepherds of Bethlehem to the Christmas angel with her long white gown, silvery wings, and halo. Also popular for children in school plays and church pageants are the royal costumes of the Three Wise Men, who journeyed from the East bearing gifts for the baby Jesus. In Germany, Christkinder (Christ Children)—girls dressed as angels, with long, filmy white veils covering their faces—walk through the neighborhoods passing out Christmas gifts to children.

Christmas mumming, or dressing in costumes and going from house to house entertaining with simple skits, is an old Christmas tradition that is still popular in some parts of the world. A unique Christmas custom in parts of Portugal is the Festas dos Rapazes, in which teenage boys wear devilish-looking masks and costumes made of multicolored strips of cloth. They parade through the community handing out gifts and performing plays. Afterward, they remove their masks and attend mass.

Foods, Recipes

The Christmas feast may include almost any type of food, depending on the country and its traditions, but certain foods are especially associated with Christmas.

A postman dressed as Santa Claus carries a stack of letters and boxes to be delivered on Christmas Day 1997. Reproduced by permission of AP/Wide World Photos.

One is a special meat dish, such as turkey, ham, or fish; another is a special drink, such as punch, eggnog, or hot tea; and a third is a special sweet or dessert, like pudding, pie or cake, cookies, or fruit. All of these Christmas foods had their beginnings hundreds of years ago.

Snout and feathers on a platter

A very old winter feast in England centered around a roast boar's head, which, in wealthy homes, servants carried to the table on a huge platter. Hunters and musicians paraded into the dining hall behind them. The boar often had a lemon, the symbol of plenty, in its mouth and greenery laced around it. People continued to purchase a boar's head for the Christmas table into the late 1800s. Today, ham and sausages are among Christmas main meat dishes.

Another old tradition was serving a baked peacock, arranged on a platter with its colorful feathers in full spread. From this tradition grew the custom of serving roast chicken, goose, and, in early America, turkey at the Christmas feast.

Mincemeat pie was another food that early Europeans traditionally served at Christmas. During the Crusades, religious wars of the eleventh, twelfth, and thirteenth centuries, soldiers brought back spices from the Middle East. These spices were used to flavor a special pie made from many kinds of meat, cooked and chopped into small pieces. The pies were often baked in oblong shapes to resemble a manger, and a baby Jesus figure was placed on top. Today, mincemeat pie is made from chopped apples and other fruits, raisins, and sweet spices.

In southern Europe and in Scandinavia, fish and other seafood were part of the Christmas feast. That tradition continues today, with many people also serving exotic varieties, such as eel, squid, and octopus. Roast pig and meat-filled pies are popular Christmas feast dishes in Asia and Latin America. Other meats, like beef and chicken, are favored in Africa.

Stir-Up Sunday and plum pudding

Plum pudding is a traditional Christmas food that also originated in England, where it was considered a delicious first course for the feast. The first plum pud-

dings, called plum pottages, were made from animal fat, bread crumbs, prunes, raisins, liquor, and spices and were served cold. People started to prepare plum pottage on the last Sunday before Advent, which was called Stir-Up Sunday. Stir-Up Sunday was the final day on which one could make the Christmas fruit cakes and puddings that require time to age before serving.

Silver coins and other charms were added to the pudding mixture, and whoever found the charms on their plate at Christmas would have good luck during the coming year. Plum pudding—which is not really made with plums—eventually evolved into a hot, breaded, fruity, spicy dessert that is still popular today in Great Britain, Ireland, and Canada.

Be of good health!

The Christmas punch served today had its origins in the old English wassail (pronounced WOSS-uhl), from the Anglo-Saxon words meaning "be of good health." In early England, wassail was made from ale, which is a type of beer, roasted apples, sugar, eggs, nutmeg, cloves, and ginger; it was served hot. The Scandinavian people had a similar drink, called glogg, which is a hot, spicy, fruity red wine still popular today. In Germany, a Christmas drink called *glühwein* (pronounced GLOO-wine) also mingles spices with hot red wine. In early America, hot apple cider replaced wassail.

An all-time favorite Christmas drink, eggnog, was created in America. It was probably a combination of the German *biersuppe* (pronounced beer-ZOO-puh), an eggy beer, and the French beverage *lait de poule* (pronounced layduhPOOL), a blend of egg yolks, milk, and sugar. Americans added nutmeg, cinnamon, and cloves, and an alcoholic drink such as brandy or rum to create eggnog. Today, this popular drink is also made without the alcohol and can be found in most supermarkets during the Christmas season.

Tree ornaments that were good to eat

Long ago, cookies were used for decorating the Christmas tree. In early America, the Pennsylvania Dutch, who were German-speaking immigrants who settled in Pennsylvania in the eighteenth century, made Christmas cookies famous. They baked them in the shapes of stars, rabbits, deer, and dolls. Today, it is still a tradition to cut out cookie dough in many shapes and bake them. After they are baked, however, they are usually decorated with icing and colored sugar, not to be hung on the tree, but to be eaten during the Christmas festivities.

Many of the early Pennsylvania Dutch cookies were made from ginger-bread. Ginger was first brought to Europe during the Middle Ages. A sweet bread made with this spice soon became popular. By the fifteenth century, it was called "gingerbread," made famous in France and Germany. Gingerbread houses and gingerbread men became associated with Christmas during the nineteenth century, and they remain a favorite of the season.

Arts, Crafts, Games

Perhaps no other time of year provides so many opportunities to be creative as Christmas. It is especially a time for decorating city streets, homes, ornaments, Christmas cards, wrapping paper, and even gifts. In

A Christmas market at Frankfurt, Germany, dates back to 1393 and still thrives today. Christmas markets are the perfect places to find handmade Christmas crafts of all kinds. Reproduced by permission of AP/Wide World Photos.

some countries, decorating for Christmas can be as simple as putting together a wreath of evergreens, holly, and ribbons. It can also be as complex as the elaborate *pesebres* in Venezuela, scenes featuring the Nativity that are worked on by whole families.

Christmas markets

In countries throughout the world, the perfect places to find handmade Christmas crafts of all kinds are the Christmas markets. These are usually rows of temporary booths set up in large market squares for artisans and craftsmen to sell their holiday wares. Shoppers will also find traditional foods and plays, live music, and puppet shows.

One of Italy's most famous crafts fairs, in the Piazza Navona in Rome, is open during the days before Epiphany, the biggest gift-giving day in Italy. Here, gifts, toys, and sweets are piled high for holiday shoppers. Equally well known is the Christmas market at Bolzano, where every imaginable Christmas decoration can be found, along with hundreds of other items. Via San Gregorio Armeno, in Naples, Italy, is famous for its crafts market featuring everything needed to create a home Nativity scene. Naples is world famous for its Nativity scenes and figures.

Germany is famous for its Christmas markets at Nuremberg, Munich, Hamburg, Bremen, and Frankfurt, where traditional foods and pastries are as numerous as the crafts. The Christkindlesmarkt in Nuremberg has been held since 1697 and draws thousands of shoppers during the three weeks before Christmas. Munich's market is the oldest; it has been held each Christmas for about six hundred years.

Hundreds of Christmas crafts markets are set up in the United States in ethnic communities or neighborhoods, in large cities, and in small towns. For example, in New York City's Ukrainian community in Manhattan, called Little Ukraine, bazaars, workshops, and art exhibits show off Ukrainian folk arts, paintings, embroidery, and holiday foods.

Christmas parades

Christmas parades also feature works of art. The large characters and floats created for these events take time and skill and many materials; they also bring joy to millions of people during the Christmas season. Among the most famous of the large Christmas parades are the Macy's Thanksgiving Day Parade, held in New York City on Thanksgiving Day to begin the Christmas shopping season, and the similar Gimbel's Department Store parade held in Philadelphia, Pennsylvania, also on Thanksgiving Day.

Symbols

Just as Christmas is celebrated in many lands and in many cultures, so too are there many symbols associated with the Christmas season. Some of them include the Nativity scene, which depicts the birth of Jesus; Santa Claus and his predecessor, Saint Nicholas; the Christmas tree, which has origins from thousands of years ago; and the ever-popular candy cane.

The Nativity scene

Because the story of Jesus' birth is at the heart of the Christmas season, many cultures have adopted the practice of depicting the scene of his birth. The Nativity scene is called the *presepio* in Italian; *crèche* in French; and *Nacimiento* in Spanish. It consists of a stable with the Christ child lying in a manger; his mother and father, Mary and Joseph; angels; the shepherds to whom the angel of the Lord announced Jesus' birth; the cattle who were housed in the stable; and the Three Wise Men, who came bearing gifts for the Christ child.

These basic figures may be joined by any number of others. The stable scene may also include the town of Bethlehem, where Jesus was born, the surrounding countryside, and the inn next to the stable.

The first Nativity figures made for home Nativity scenes were made of bread dough, wax, or spun glass, and the backgrounds often resembled a paradise, with beautiful flowers, waterfalls, and animals.

Today, Nativity scenes often reproduce the birth of Jesus using the scenery and costumes of the country in which they are made. For example, some Italian artisans create Nativity scenes in which the figures are clothed in costumes of nineteenth-century Naples. In some parts of Africa, Nativity scenes are homemade and look like poor neighborhoods, complete with garbage and stagnant pools.

Many Nativity scenes are live—that is, they use real people and animals and a background that looks like a real stable. These Nativities are often performed as part of a church play or pageant at Christmas. Live presepi have been popular in Italy for hundreds of years. In the 1600s, one ruler created a Nativity with one thousand shepherds.

The manger tradition: In Catholic churches, the figure of the infant Jesus is usually placed in the manger crib during midnight mass on Christmas Eve; many families place his figure in their home Nativity scenes before going to mass. Nativity scenes are often displayed throughout the Christmas season until Epiphany, January 6, when the Three Wise Men are believed to have found the Christ child in the manger.

Santa Claus

Santa Claus—the "right jolly old elf" with a long white beard, dressed in a red suit with white trim—has a long history and many names. According to legend, he travels around the world from his home at

A Humble Birth in a Stable

An Italian priest, Saint Francis of Assisi (c. 1182–1226), is said to have had the first idea for a Nativity scene. In 1223, he created a presepio in a small monastery made of caves in the mountain town of Gréccio, Italy. Saint Francis's presepio was a live scene, with a real manger and hay, farm animals, and real people dressed as Mary and Joseph and the shepherds. A life-size wax figure represented the baby Jesus. Saint Francis wanted to re-create the night of Jesus' birth and make it come alive for the people of his village. He invited the villagers, who came throughout the night carrying torches to see the first reenactment of the Nativity.

the North Pole in a sleigh pulled by flying reindeer and drops down chimneys, leaving toys for children on Christmas Eve. Santa Claus is one of the foremost symbols of Christmas, but he is also a Christmas legend—one that has changed over the many years since he came into being.

The real Saint Nick: The legend of Santa Claus began with Saint Nicholas, a fourth-century bishop of the city of Myra, in the land that is now Turkey. Nicholas is said to have been the son of wealthy parents who died when he was a boy. He inherited their wealth but gave it away to the poor.

Saint Nicholas is said to have performed many miracles to help children. He became the patron saint of children, sailors,

Sinterklaas, the Netherlands' version of Saint Nicholas, rides through the streets of the small Dutch village of Hattum in 1999. Saint Nicholas, the patron saint of children, sailors, merchants, bakers, and virgins, is also known as a giver of unexpected gifts. Reproduced by permission of AP/Wide World Photos.

(pronounced SIN-ter-kloss), to America in the 1700s when they settled in New York. They continued to honor him on December 6 in their most important winter holiday, Saint Nicholas Day. On Christmas Eve, Dutch families honored the Christ child, who they called Christkindl. Children believed he came riding on a mule and passed through the keyhole of each home.

As English settlers came to New York, Sinterklaas became Saint Claas, and then Santa Claus. The name for the Christ child also changed, with Christkindl becoming Kriss Kringle. Eventually the two legends combined into one and came to resemble other European folklore characters who were associated with the spirit of giving.

Santa Claus around the world: Santa Claus and figures similar to him are part of the Christmas holiday in many countries. In England, children call him Father Christmas. In France, he is Pere Noël (pronounced PAIR no-EL; Father Noël), who looks much like the American Santa and leaves gifts in children's wooden shoes on Christmas Eve.

In Sweden, he is Jultomten (pronounced yool-TOM-ten), a little old gnome with a long white beard. In Finland, he is Joulupukki (pronounced yool-uh-POO-kee), the Christmas goat, who sometimes comes on a bicycle and sometimes dressed as Santa Claus, in a sled drawn by real reindeer. Children in Iceland believe in thirteen mischievous little elves called the Yuletide Lads, who come one at a time beginning thirteen days before Christmas Eve, and leave little gifts each day.

In Italy, San Nicola (Saint Nicholas), is a beloved saint who leaves a special sweet

merchants, bakers, and virgins and also became known as a giver of unexpected gifts. Saint Nicholas's feast day was celebrated by the Eastern Orthodox Church on December 6, the anniversary of his death. He was one of the most loved of the saints, especially in Greece, Russia, Sicily, Germany, Austria, Switzerland, Italy, and Holland.

Santa comes to America: Dutch immigrants introduced Saint Nicholas, or Sinterklaas treat called *torrone* (pronounced tor-ROH-nay) in good children's shoes on the eve of his feast day, December 6. Italians also honor Babbo Natale (pronounced bob-boh nuh-TAH-lay), Father Christmas. But it is La Befana, the Christmas witch, who brings gifts to the children. She comes on January 5, the eve of Epiphany. Befana's Russian counterpart is Babouschka (pronounced bah-BOOSH-kuh), the Christmas witch, or the more modern Grandfather Frost, who, with his niece, the Snow Maiden, passes out presents on New Year's Day.

In Germany, Santa Claus is Weihnachtsmann (pronounced WEE-nokstman), Christmas Man. In Japan, the gift bearer is a priest called Hoteiosho (pronounced ho-tay-OH-sho), who delivers presents on Christmas Eve and has eyes in the back of his head to watch children's behavior. In Latin America, the Three Kings give gifts to children on the eve of Epiphany, and the Christ Child or Santa Claus leaves gifts on Christmas Day.

The Christmas tree

There are many legends that tell the origin of the Christmas tree. According to one, Martin Luther (1483–1546), a German priest who worked to make reforms in the Catholic Church, was out walking one clear winter night when he saw an evergreen tree framed by twinkling stars. Luther thought the sight was so beautiful that he cut down a tree, took it home, and fastened candles to its branches to show his family.

During the 1300s to 1500s, a play performed each December 24 in Europe told the biblical story of Adam and Eve and featured a fir tree to represent the Tree of the Knowledge of Good and Evil, or the Tree of Life, in the Garden of Eden. The tree was decorated with apples and placed inside a circle of candles.

By the early 1600s, people in Germany had begun to combine the Paradise tree with their Christmas custom of decorating a pyramid-shaped wooden frame with evergreen branches. This first Christmas tree—called Christbaum, tree of Christ—was decorated with lighted candles, fruit, nuts, candies, Communion wafers, and paper roses representing the Virgin Mary, the mother of Jesus.

German immigrants to Pennsylvania brought the Christmas tree custom with them in the early 1800s. These trees were decorated with homemade gingerbread cookies in the shape of stars, animals, houses, and diamonds and with dried apples, raisins, paper flowers, and flannel ribbons. Some groups made more impressive ornaments and sold tickets to people who came to see their finely decorated Christmas trees.

The Victorian "family Christmas": In 1841, British queen Victoria's husband, Prince Albert (1819–1861), who was born in Germany, had a tree brought from his homeland and set up at Windsor Castle, where he lived with Queen Victoria (1819–1901) and their children. The royal Christmas tree became a model for all of England, and Victoria and Albert transformed Christmas from a time of feasting, drinking, and gambling to a family-centered holiday.

In 1850, the popular U.S. magazine *Godey's Lady's Book* printed a copy of a drawing of the British royal family gathered around their Christmas tree. From that time on, the decorated tree became a Christmas symbol desired by every American family.

They adorned the trees with candles, Santa Claus figures made of cotton or wood, flowers, apples, cookies, popcorn, candies, tinsel, toys, and the family's Christmas gifts.

A string of lights and two dozen silver balls: Soon after the electric light bulb was invented in 1879, families began to have electric Christmas tree lights. The first were single bulbs in many shapes. Before long, the bulbs could be made to blink off and on, and then strings of colored lights became available.

The first tree ornaments for sale were made by glass blowers in Germany. These became available in U.S. department stores in the late 1800s, but they cost more than the average person could afford. By the middle of the twentieth century, however, Christmas ornaments, lights, and other decorations were widely available and priced so that almost everyone could buy them.

In addition to lights, the most popular decorations for the Christmas tree are a star or angel for the top; gold, silver, or colored balls; tinsel that hangs like icicles from the branches; candy canes; red ribbons; and Santa Claus, reindeer, and elf figures. Each country in which the tree is part of the Christmas celebration has its own traditional tree trimmings. For example, in Sweden and Norway, straw ornaments in the shape of stars and animals are popular, as are miniature flags of many countries.

The candy cane

The all-time favorite traditional Christmas candy, the candy cane, is the subject of many legends. Its origin is uncertain, but it is said to have been a favorite of children as early as 1670, when a German choirmaster had sugar sticks bent into the shape of shepherds' staffs for his young singers. Another legend says a candymaker who lived in England during the late 1700s molded white candy into a shepherd's staff and decorated it with red stripes to represent the blood of Christ, shed for the forgiveness of human sin.

Music, Dance

"Jesus, Light of All the Nations," is considered the earliest song written to honor the birth of Christ. It was written around the time Christmas was first celebrated, by Saint Hilary Poitiers, who died in 368.

Most early hymns were formal and religious, and most were in Latin, the language of the Church. Saint Francis of Assisi, a thirteenth-century Italian priest, started the custom of creating songs about Christ and the Bible that the common people could understand. As ministers to the poor in many countries, Saint Francis and his fellow priests asked composers to write songs about the birth of Christ that could be sung by people in their own languages in their own homes and in the streets. Their idea was accepted all over Europe, and a number of carols were written in German, French, and English during the fourteenth and fifteenth centuries.

Christmas carols and caroling

The words of many Christmas carols come from Chapters 1 and 2 of the Gospel of Luke, the third book of the New Testament of the Holy Bible. Carols are both joyful and reverent; many are set to melodies taken from the most well-known works of classical composers. For example, "Joy to the World," written by English hymn writer Isaac Watts in 1719, is set to a

Members of the Chicago Children's Choir sing in downtown Chicago, Illinois, in 1999. Caroling as a custom began in France and England during the Middle Ages. Reproduced by permission of AP/Wide World Photos.

melody composed by Lowell Mason, but it was taken from the famous oratorio (a long choral piece without action or scenery) *The Messiah,* by British composer George Frideric Handel (1685–1759). "Hark! the Herald Angels Sing" was written by English religious leader Charles Wesley in 1737, with a melody adapted from German composer Felix Mendelssohn (1809–1847).

Most of the favorite carols of today were written in the 1700s and 1800s and have endured as Christmas classics. Perhaps the most well-known Christmas carol is "Silent Night, Holy Night," said to have been written in 1818 by Austrian minister Joseph Mohr after the church organ broke down and could not be repaired in time for midnight mass on Christmas Eve. His friend Franz Gruber, an organist, quickly composed the music, and the two surprised the congregation with the beautiful new song.

Caroling as a custom began in France and England during the Middle Ages. At first, carolers were groups of men and boys, called "waits," who sang from door to door for money or their supper. Later, singers walked from house to house in the cold, stopping outside each door to entertain. They were invited in for drinks and snacks.

The old custom was introduced to the United States in the early 1900s in Boston, where the first organized Christmas caroling took place. Today, groups of carolers, both young and old, entertain families from door to door or sing in hospitals, nursing homes, shopping malls, and schools during the Christmas season.

Classical music and ballet

Famous Christmas classical music pieces include Handel's *The Messiah,* composed in 1742, and Russian composer Peter Tchaikovsky's (1840–1893) ballet *The Nutcracker.*

The theme of *The Messiah* is taken from the Bible and focuses on hope, suffering, death, and resurrection. It was performed at Easter during Handel's lifetime, but is now performed mainly at Christmas. *The Nutcracker,* composed in 1892, is a ballet about a girl whose Christmas fantasies come true when a toy nutcracker comes to life. It is performed by local ballet companies in nearly every U.S. city during the Christmas season.

Ethiopia

Name of Holiday: Genna or Gannā

Introduction

Christmas in Ethiopia is called *Genna,* which comes from the ancient Greek word *jevva,* meaning "nativity" or "birth."

Genna is also the name of a popular hockey-like game that is played on this holiday.

Because Ethiopia uses the Julian calendar, Christmas is celebrated on January 7, as it is in the Eastern Orthodox Church. The Julian calendar is thirteen days behind the Gregorian calendar, which was first introduced in the 1500s and continues to be used today by most countries. Epiphany, called Timqat, is celebrated on January 19 and is, by far, the bigger celebration.

History

Christianity was introduced into the area of northeastern Africa that is now Ethiopia, formerly called Abyssinia, in about 330 by Frumentius, a Christian bishop from Syria. During the seventh century, Christianity in Ethiopia was influenced by the Coptic Christian Church of neighboring Egypt. The Coptic Church originated in Egypt nearly two thousand years ago with the Copts, who believe that Jesus Christ, the founder of Christianity, was always divine, even in his human form.

Christianity was threatened in northeastern Africa as the Islamic religion became widespread from the seventh century onward, but today about 40 percent of Ethiopians remain Christian. These Orthodox Christians still practice their faith in much the same way as the early Coptic Christians did, with many Old Testament traditions.

Folklore, Legends, Stories

An interesting legend surrounds the origin of the hockey-like game genna. Ethiopians say that the shepherds watching their flocks in the field when the angel of the Lord announced Jesus' birth were playing the game as they guarded their sheep. According to another version of the story, the shepherds began to wave their staffs and play when they heard the good news that Jesus was born (see "Arts, Crafts, Games").

Customs, Traditions, Ceremonies

Many of the Christmas customs of the Western world, such as giving gifts, decorating the home, and celebrating Santa Claus, are not kept by Ethiopian Christians. Today, however, some churches have adopted the practice of putting up Christmas trees and gift-giving is sometimes practiced, with children receiving small presents. Christmas Day is celebrated with a special early morning church service; the men and boys spend the rest of the day playing genna. The biggest celebration occurs at Epiphany, about two weeks after Christmas.

Special church service

Ethiopian Christians rise early for a special church service on Genna. This service begins at 3 A.M. Coptic priests wearing beautiful ceremonial robes, and accompanied by the beat of ceremonial drums, form a procession along with poets and singers. The chants and songs are in an ancient language called Geez, which is used only in church.

The priests carry prayer sticks and rattles. The sticks are long and crutch-like and are used to tap out a rhythm for the ceremonial dances that begin after the march into the church. The priests also lean on the prayer sticks when they become tired. The Genna service continues until about 9 A.M.

The Church of San Jorge, one of the churches Lalibela built in Roha, Ethiopia. The emperor had eleven churches built here; famous writings claim that visiting the churches is like seeing the face of Jesus Christ. Reproduced by permission of the Corbis Corporation (Bellevue).

Christmas pilgrimage

Each year on Genna, thousands of Ethiopian Christians journey to a holy city in Ethiopia called Lalibela. This city is named for an early Ethiopian emperor, Lalibela, who ruled from about 1185 to 1225. Originally the capital city of Roha, Lalibela is home to eleven churches that the emperor built to make the city look like the Christian holy city of Jerusalem. Famous writings called the *Acts of Lalibela* claim that visiting the churches here is like seeing the face of Christ.

The churches are carved out of the area's volcanic rock formations and took many years to complete. Lalibela brought thousands of craftsmen and workers from as far away as Egypt and the Holy Land to carve them. Each of the eleven churches is different, but all have remarkable designs, with pillars, windows, altars, and passageways connecting the various structures. Roha was renamed Lalibela after the ruler's death, and since the thirteenth century, it has been a place of pilgrimage for Coptic Christians in Ethiopia.

On the eve of Genna, thousands of pilgrims wait on the hillsides surrounding the city for the procession at dawn, which signals the beginning of the religious services. A long line of priests, monks, and nuns make up the procession. They walk to the top of the highest hill, chanting.

Four men carry the *tabot,* or the church's symbolic representation of the Ark of the Covenant. The Ark of the Covenant is described in the Bible in Exodus 25:10–22 as a chest that is said to hold the tablets on which God wrote his Ten Commandments for the prophet Moses. The Ten Commandments are the basic laws about how people should treat each other and what their duties are to God. The tabot is a holy symbol for every Ethiopian Christian church; each church has its own, and these are usually highly decorated with gold and precious stones.

After the procession, the priests, wearing colored robes, dance, as they do in Christian churches throughout Ethiopia. A great feast follows the dance, and people play games until dusk.

Blessing the waters at Epiphany

In Western churches, Epiphany commemorates the visit of the Three Wise Men who brought gifts to the Christ child. In Eastern churches, however, it is the occasion for celebrating Jesus' baptism in the river Jordan. The Ethiopian Epiphany is celebrated on January 19 and is called Timqat, which means "baptism." To Ethiopians, Timqat is a more important holiday than Christmas, or Genna.

On the eve of Timqat, people put on clean, white robes and gather at the nearest stream or pool. The local church's tabot, or copy of the Ark of the Covenant, is carried to the stream. After supper at home, the people return to the stream, where they sing and dance until it is time for a special mass, which begins at about 2 A.M.

At dawn, the priests bless the waters of the stream and sprinkle those gathered to worship so that they can renew their Christian vows. Some people are baptized; others bathe in the blessed waters. Local dignitaries and government officials might also attend the Timqat service.

At noon, a colorful procession of priests, followed by the worshipers, escorts the tabot back to the church. Along the way, the priests dance; others march and chant. Children run and play, following the crowd. After the Ark is safely back in the church, everyone goes home for a holiday feast.

On the following day, Ethiopians celebrate the Feast of Saint Michael, who in the Orthodox religion is said to be a prince and the greatest of all the angels. Drinking holy water and bathing in hot springs to help cure disease are some of the rituals performed on Saint Michael's Day.

An ancient warrior game

An Ethiopian national sporting event called *yeferas guks* is often held during the afternoon of Timqat. Young men dress as ancient warriors in capes and headdresses made from lions' manes and battle one another on horseback, by throwing bamboo lances. They protect themselves with shields made from hippopotamus, or other animal, hides.

The young warriors display excellent horsemanship; the horses are also decked out in finery. Centuries ago, survival in this type of battle depended solely on the rider's skill, because there was no armor to protect him and the javelins used were extremely sharp and deadly.

Clothing, Costumes

The priests' robes worn at Genna and at Timqat are brilliantly colored, in combinations of violet, gold, and green, or red, gold, and blue, and are made of velvet, silks, and woven cotton. They are worn with white head coverings called turbans. On Timqat, children wear new clothes they have been given for the occasion. Adults wash their robes, or *shammā,* and women dress up in their finest costumes.

Foods, Recipes

On Genna, a feast is held after the ceremonies in Lalibela. Crowds that have come for the church services are often fed bread and mead, a type of fermented beverage made with honey, that the priests have blessed. Later, the men sometimes feast on raw meat.

An Ethiopian priest wearing a brilliantly colored silk robe and a white turban. Each year on Genna, Coptic priests wear their ceremonial robes and, accompanied by the beat of ceremonial drums, form a procession. Reproduced by permission of Cory Langley.

Ethiopians like lamb, chicken, goat, and beef, but do not eat pork, and eat only a small amount of fish. Many of the traditional foods are spicy stews with meat and vegetables. Such a stew is considered the national dish of Ethiopia. The spiciest are called *wats,* and the same dish with less spice is called *alecha.* These stews are served with rice and yogurt.

A grain called teff is grown in Ethiopia and is used to make a flat bread called *injera,* which serves as table, utensil, and food. During a meal, a large flat-topped basket called a *mesob* is placed on the floor or table, and everyone gathers around it in a circle. Injera is laid across the top of the basket and food is placed on top of the bread. Diners break off a piece of injera with their fingers and use it to scoop up the food.

Lentils and other legumes, such as peas and beans, are important crops in Ethiopia. Bean salads are often eaten as side dishes or as main dishes on occasions when the Church forbids the eating of meat.

Arts, Crafts, Games

Among the most highly decorative craftsmanship in Ethiopia is the making of cloth and clothing. Ethiopians weave by hand cotton cloth with detailed patterns and embroider clothing and other items with intricate designs in bright colors. They also wear silks and brocaded velvets.

During the Genna and Timqat celebrations, and for all Coptic Christian religious processions, the priests use brightly colored umbrellas that resemble flowers. These are decorated with intricate embroidery and fringes. During the processions, celebrants also carry intricately designed Coptic crosses, some of which are very old.

Gold is mined in Ethiopia, and for centuries the people have used it to create religious objects for the churches, such as golden goblets used to offer water blessed during Timqat. A copy of the Ark of the Covenant, which represents God's covenant with Moses' people in the biblical Old Testament, is found in most churches. Gold and jewels adorn the replicas. Ethiopi-

ans also use gold to make plates and sheets for binding sacred books.

The Christmas game

The game that makes up the biggest part of Christmas celebrations in Ethiopia is called, like the holiday itself, genna, or *ko-lee.* It is played outdoors with a wooden puck or leather ball and special curved sticks. Two teams are formed on the day of the game, often representing rivalry between villages. Teams are made up of young men and boys and sometimes older men.

Genna is a fast, rough game that can leave players with cuts, bruises, and broken bones. As in hockey, the players try to get the puck or ball across a goal line. The game can be played on an open field or on a street in town. The players let out their aggression on this day, and at the end of the game—which lasts all afternoon until dusk—the winners make up rude rhymes to shout at the losers. Then the winners visit house after house in the village, where they are welcomed with refreshments and gifts.

Making the genna stick

The sticks used in the traditional Ethiopian game of genna are made by each boy or man who intends to play the game on Christmas Day. Around the end of November, each player goes into the woods to cut a special young tree with a knobby root, or a branch with a bump where it joins the tree trunk. The young man strips the bark from his sapling or branch and shapes the root or knob into a head for the genna stick, somewhat like the head of a golf club. The stick is then dried and rubbed with oil to keep it from becoming brittle and cracking or breaking. The genna puck is also made from a knobby root, or sometimes from hard leather.

Music, Dance

Although instruments that make melodies are not used during Genna, a type of rhythmic music accompanies the special dances performed by priests at the church services. Skin-covered drums called *kabaro* provide the basis of the rhythm, and the priests' rattles, called *sistra,* or *tsenatsel,* add to the beat. The pear-shaped rattles have rows of metal rods strung with metal discs that jingle when they are shaken. The priests also tap a rhythm with their wooden prayer sticks, called *makamiya.* The traditional hymn sung by the Coptic priests at the Genna service is called "Mahlet."

For More Information

Berg, Elizabeth. *Ethiopia: Festivals of the World.* Milwaukee, Wis.: Gareth Stevens, 1999.

Fradin, Dennis Brindell. *Ethiopia: Enchantment of the World.* Chicago, Ill.: Children's Press, 1994.

Web sites

"Christmas in Ethiopia." [Online] http://www.lhmint.org/christmas/ethiopia.html (accessed on January 26, 2000).

"Santa's Favorites Around the World: Christmas in Ethiopia." [Online] http://www.santas.net/ethiopianchristmas.htm (accessed on January 26, 2000).

Italy

Name of Holiday: Il Natale

Introduction

Christmas, or Il Natale (pronounced eel nah-TAH-lay; The Birthday), has always been a holiday strongly connected to the Roman Catholic Church in Italy. Most celebrations center around special masses, including the midnight mass on Christmas Eve. The Nativity scene, or *presepio,* is central to the observance of Christmas in Italian homes, and placing the figure of the Gesu Bambino, the infant Jesus, in the manger on Christmas Eve highlights the quiet festivities.

History

Christians began to celebrate the birth of Jesus Christ on December 25 in about A.D. 336, in Rome, Italy, during the rule of Emperor Constantine the Great (ruled 306–37). They called this early festival the Feast of the Nativity.

By the end of the fourth century, Christianity had become the official religion of the Roman Empire, and the celebration of the Nativity was extended to the Eastern Church in Constantinople (now Istanbul, Turkey) and then to Egypt by 432. By the time Christmas became established throughout Europe, in the thirteenth century, it was already centuries old in Italy.

During the thirteenth century, an Italian priest, Saint Francis of Assisi (c. 1182–1226), helped establish two important Christmas traditions that would find their way throughout the world. He was the first to create a Nativity scene, or presepio, depicting the birth of Christ in a stable. It was also at Saint Francis's suggestion that the first Christmas carols were written for the common people, rather than in Latin, the language of the Catholic Church.

During the fourteenth and fifteenth centuries, many of the traditions associated with Epiphany began. Epiphany is an important part of the Christmas holiday season in Italy. It also marks the beginning of the Carnival season. Italian men would dress up in witch costumes, imitating La Befana, the witch who is said to leave presents for children on Epiphany. They roamed the streets and stormed into the Christmas marketplaces, yelling and making merry. Children once formed a procession dressed in costumes of the Three Kings and went from house to house asking for small presents or food. Today, this custom is still popular in some areas.

In Renaissance times, especially during the 1500s and 1600s, many events took place that affected Christianity. Saint Peter's Basilica, headquarters of the Roman Catholic Church and home of the pope, the church's leader, was built. Carnival and Christmas customs were started, including the tradition of holding an Epiphany procession by torchlight that ends with the lighting of a bonfire and exploding firecrackers. The goose game, popular at Christmas to this day, was invented (see "Customs, Traditions, Ceremonies"), and many of the traditional Christmas foods, such as spicy, nutty raisin breads, were created in Italian kitchens.

It was during the 1500s that Roman Catholic Church missionaries, many from Spain, began to spread the Christian religion to the New World. They introduced the native cultures to the elaborate rituals of the Catholic Church, especially the dramatic customs associated with Christmas. Such traditions were embraced by many people in Latin America.

Folklore, Legends, Stories

There are many stories associated with Il Natale in Italy, but none is so popular as the legend of La Befana.

The Christmas witch

In Italy, children believe it is La Befana, the good witch, and not Santa Claus, who brings them gifts. And, unlike Santa, La Befana does not come on Christmas Eve or Christmas Day. Instead, she visits on January 5, the eve of the Feast of Epiphany, or the twelfth day of Christmas. La Befana's name comes from the Greek word *epiphaneia,* meaning "appearance" or "manifestation." She makes her appearance on Epiphany to commemorate the visit by the Three Wise Men to the Christ child.

According to legend, the Three Wise Men, who traveled to Bethlehem bearing gifts for the baby Jesus, stopped at Befana's house on their way. They asked her to go with them to see the newborn child, but Befana said she could not go because she had so much housecleaning to finish. She told them she would follow when she was done. But the night sky had clouded over when she set out, and Befana could not find the bright star the wise men had told her would guide her to Jesus.

The old woman regretted her decision to clean house and miss such an important event and has been sorry ever since. So, on Epiphany Eve, she flies on her broomstick to every house, leaving gifts for children and searching for a glimpse of the

An Italian nun on a pilgrimage to Bethlehem lies over the grotto where Christian tradition states that Jesus was born. Reproduced by permission of AP/Wide World Photos.

Christ child. If children have been good, they are rewarded with toys and candies in their stockings; if they have not, they sometimes get garlic and lumps of a dark, sugary candy that looks like coal. La Befana takes the form of either a kindly old woman or an evil, ugly witch with a black face, depending on whether children have been good or bad during the year.

Other Italian Christmas figures

Like the French, English, and Germans, Italians tell legends of a Father Christmas or Santa Claus figure. In Italian, his name is Babbo Natale, and he, like La Befana, is sometimes said to give gifts to good children, but on Christmas Eve.

Influenced by the Roman Catholic Church, many Italian children believe it is Gesù Bambino, or Baby Jesus, who leaves them gifts on Christmas Eve. He was once thought to travel from house to house on a donkey. Young children sometimes write letters to Baby Jesus telling him what they would like for Christmas.

San Nicola (Saint Nicholas) is still a beloved saint in Italy, and he is said to leave a special sweet treat called *torrone* in good children's shoes on the eve of his feast day,

December 6. Many children also expect small gifts from Saint Lucia on the eve of her feast day, December 13 (see "Honoring Saint Lucia" under "Customs, Traditions, Ceremonies").

Customs, Traditions, Ceremonies

Most Italians celebrate the Christmas season beginning with Advent, the four-week period associated with the coming of Christ. Christmas fairs during Advent feature fireworks, bonfires, and Christmas sweets. Christmas begins in Rome on December 8, the Feast of the Immaculate Conception. On this day, the fire department, acting for the pope, drapes flowers around the statue of Jesus' mother, Mary, which sits high on a column at the Piazza di Spagna (Spanish Square).

In many small towns, people celebrate the Nine Days of Christmas, or Novena di Natale, which includes Christmas Day and the preceding eight days, by attending church services. Children sometimes go from house to house reciting Christmas rhymes; the residents give them money or treats.

Honoring Santa Lucia

Sicily is the home of Saint Lucy, a fourth-century Christian martyr who was punished for her religious beliefs. Although little is known of her life, some accounts say she lost her sight while being tortured, or that she blinded herself to protest the cruel treatment of Christians. She is known as the patron saint of the blind. The name Lucy comes from the Latin words *lux* and *lucis,* meaning "light."

Legend holds that in 1582 Lucy brought a ship full of wheat to the famine-stricken people of Palermo and Syracuse, much like a Swedish legend of rescue from starvation around the same time. To this day, each of the two southeastern Italian cities claims the miracle for its own. To show respect for Lucy, Italians eat nothing made of wheat flour on her special day.

For hundreds of years, Italians have celebrated Santa Lucia's (pronounced loo-CHEE-uh; Saint Lucy) Day by lighting bonfires or marching in processions by torchlight. In Palermo, a special dessert called *cuccia* (rhymes with Lucia) is made of whole wheat berries and sweetened ricotta cheese flavored with orange and chocolate.

Many Italian children believe that it is Saint Lucy who leaves gifts for them, rather than La Befana. She is said to travel on a donkey on the eve of December 13, bearing presents, coins, sweets, or flowers. Children leave hay, carrots, or bowls of milk for her donkey. Some children write letters to Lucy, just as children in other countries write to Santa Claus.

La Vigilia: Christmas Eve traditions

Because it is the eve of Jesus' birth, Christmas Eve, or La Vigilia in Italian, is the biggest day of the season for celebrating. According to Roman Catholic tradition, it is a day of fasting from red meat, so the Italian Christmas Eve dinner is prepared around fish courses, with eel being the most popular. A three- or four-foot-long adult female eel called *capitone* is considered the best type of eel for the Christmas Eve feast.

Many Italian families serve a fish dinner with seven different types of fish or seafood. Various pastas and fresh vegetables accompany the fish. Dessert consists of fruits, nuts, candies, cakes, and sweet breads.

After dinner, children often give performances by singing songs or reciting rhymes, and families play a traditional bingo-like game called *tombola*. Another traditional game is *gioco dell'oca,* "the goose game." The goose game was invented in the 1500s, and is a board game played with dice. Players take turns rolling the dice and move along a spiral race course, trying to be the first to arrive at the center of the maze.

On Christmas Eve, Italians attend a midnight mass, which begins at 10 P.M. When they return home from church, a member of the family, sometimes the youngest child, places the figure of the infant Jesus in the manger to complete the family's presepio. In some homes, the baby Jesus is placed in the manger before the La Vigilia dinner.

It is a Christmas tradition to burn a large log, called a Yule log, in Italian homes each night throughout the twelve days of Christmas. This tradition began in Scandinavia and spread to other countries in Europe. It is a custom that is still practiced in many countries. Children are sometimes blindfolded and recite poems for the Christ child; they are then given small gifts or sweets as the Yule log is lit. Ashes from the Yule log are often sprinkled on the soil to ensure its fertility in the coming year.

Pope John Paul II embraces two Polish children wearing national costumes after they presented him with a Christmas tree during the 1985 midnight Christmas mass in Saint Peter's Basilica in the Vatican City. Reproduced by permission of AP/Wide World Photos.

(pronounced pah-nay-TONE-nay), a tall loaf cake made with raisins and citron.

Il Natale: Christmas Day

Christmas Day is quiet in Italy. Families go to church and visit relatives, and enjoy a large holiday feast later in the day. The multicourse meal may include turkey, sausages, fish, pasta, veal, and goose, served with marinated and cooked vegetables. For dessert, there is fruit, nuts, and the traditional Italian cake *panettone*

The pope's Christmas address

Saint Peter's Basilica in the Vatican City (the independent papal state located within the city of Rome) is one of the most well-known churches in the world. Each year, the pope, the head of the Roman Catholic Church, holds a Christmas Eve mass inside the cathedral. On Christmas Day, thousands gather to hear his tradition-

Panettone (Christmas Fruit Bread)

Ingredients

2 packages yeast

⅓ cup water

6 cups flour

¾ cup sugar

2 sticks butter, softened

2 eggs, beaten

1 teaspoon lemon juice

1 tablespoon honey

1 tablespoon vanilla

¾ cup raisins

¾ cup glazed orange peel

¾ cup pine nuts

melted butter for brushing loaves

Directions

1. Dissolve the yeast in lukewarm water. Add 1 cup of flour and stir to make dough.
2. Shape the dough into a ball and put it into a greased bowl. Cover with a damp towel, and let it rise in a warm place for 1 hour.
3. Mix together the butter, the rest of the flour, the eggs, sugar, vanilla, and honey. Work this mixture into the dough and knead until creamy.
4. Roll the dough into a rectangle. Mix lemon juice with raisins, orange peel, and pine nuts and sprinkle mixture over dough. Fold the dough over and over, and knead until the fruit and nuts are mixed throughout.
5. Shape the dough into a ball and let rise again, covered, for 30 minutes.
6. Punch the dough down, then divide it into 3 pieces and shape each section into a ball.
7. Prepare a greased 8-inch round pan with a brown paper collar of 3 inches. Place dough in pan and cover; let rise until doubled.
8. With a knife, cut a cross shape into the top of each ball of dough. Brush the dough with melted butter.
9. Bake at 375 degrees for 50 minutes or until a toothpick inserted in the middle comes out clean, brushing once or twice with melted butter during baking.

Makes 3 panettone.

al Christmas address, "To the City and to the World" ("Urbi et Orbi"), given from the balcony of Saint Peter's, overlooking Saint Peter's Square. In recent years, it has been broadcast on radio and television to millions of people around the world.

Foods, Recipes

During the Christmas season the amount of feasting in Italy seems boundless—from the multicourse fish meal served on Christmas Eve to the array of sweets and pastries enjoyed throughout the season.

Cakes are especially popular during Christmas festivities; each region of Italy is known for a particular kind. Christmas Italian cakes include *pandoro* and panettone.

Pandoro is a cake that originated in the Italian city of Verona. According to legend, it is eaten by angels in heaven. It is a tall cake shaped like a star and sprinkled with sugar. It does not contain candied fruit, as so many Italian Christmas cakes do.

Panettone is a fruity Christmas cake that is so good it is often given as a gift. It is baked with candied fruit and may include flavored fillings and chocolate. It was originally a small cake that was packed in famous drum-shaped boxes. Eventually, it became the taller cake of today.

Arts, Crafts, Games

Creating the Nativity scene, or presepio, has become an art in Italy. Artists and craftsmen create miniature presepi made from terra-cotta (fired clay), wood, and other natural materials. Some of the figures in the Nativities are dressed in the clothing of Jesus' time, but many wear Italian costumes of the Middle Ages (about 500–1500). The presepio figurines, called *pastori,* are sold all over the world and become treasured additions to Nativity scenes in many countries.

Italians display their Nativity scenes from Christmas Eve through Epiphany, and many families add a new piece to their collection each year. In Catholic churches everywhere, the Nativity scene is unveiled just before midnight on Christmas Eve. The baby Jesus figure is placed in the manger on Christmas Eve.

Making a Presepio at Home

Ordinary household items or scraps from other crafts projects can often be recycled to make a Nativity scene. Items such as construction paper, cardboard or poster board, scraps of wood, empty thread spools, plastic bottles, cookie or bread dough, clay, fabric scraps, wallpaper, wrapping paper, and even rocks glued together can be used to make figures of people and animals.

A wooden produce box or a shoe box lined with fabric makes an excellent stable—or craft one from scrap blocks of wood or popsicle sticks. Real straw could be used in the manger and glued to the top of the stable to create a thatched roof. Houseplants or twigs snipped from evergreen trees may be added around the outside for greenery. You may also try other natural materials like pine cones, corn husks, bark chips, grapevines, and holly and mistletoe to add a realistic look.

Living presepios, life-size manger scenes with real people and animals, also herald Christmas in schools and churches throughout Italy.

The *ceppo* and the Christmas tree

Southern Italian homes often display the presepio on the bottom shelf of a *ceppo* (pronounced CHAY-poe), a triangle of shelves in a Christmas tree shape. The brightly painted wooden shelves display candles and Christmas greenery, with a star

This monumental Christmas Nativity scene featuring life-size figures decorates
Saint Peter's Square in the Vatican City. Creating the Nativity scene, or presepio, has become an art in Italy.
Reproduced by permission of AP/Wide World Photos.

or doll at the top. The ceppo is also used to hold gifts, candy, and nuts.

In northern Italy, most families decorate a Christmas tree instead of a ceppo. Markets at Christmastime stock everything necessary to decorate a tree.

Music, Dance

Music plays an important part during the Christmas season in Italy. After all, according to historians, it was Saint Francis of Assisi, a thirteenth-century Italian priest, who was responsible for commissioning the first Christmas carols.

Before Saint Francis, sacred songs were written only in Latin and could be heard only in churches. At that time, most people could not understand Latin, and many did not live near or were not able to attend church services. Saint Francis introduced the idea of Christmas carols by asking musicians to write songs about Christ and the Christmas story in the language of the common people. This practice became so popular that it was eventually accepted all over Europe.

One of the most famous Christmas carols, "O Come, All Ye Faithful," was written in Italy by an unknown author in about 1250. It is called "Adeste Fideles" in Italian, and was originally a Latin poem. In 1841, it was translated into English by clergyman Frederick Oakeley. Historians believe John Francis Wade, who lived in the middle 1700s, composed the music.

Christmas opera

Italy not only produced the first carols, it also gave birth to opera. An opera is a drama that is set to music and has little or no spoken dialogue. The first opera was written in Italy during the 1600s. The tradition spread throughout Europe, but Italy continued to dominate the form for centuries. Gian-Carlo Menotti of Italy wrote the opera *Amahl and the Night Visitors* for television. The story of the visit of the Three Wise Men, it first aired on Christmas Eve of 1951 and has become a regular part of holiday TV viewing.

Shepherds and bagpipes

Another popular Italian Christmas tradition is the coming of the *zampognari* (pronounced zom-pone-YAR-ee), or bagpipe-playing shepherds. In early times, shepherds came down from the mountainous regions around Rome and went from house to house playing and singing carols during the Advent season. Today, musicians dress in the clothing of shepherds and perform at public festivals and in parades.

For More Information

Berg, Elizabeth. *Italy: Festivals of the World*. Milwaukee, Wis.: Gareth Stevens, 1997.

Calvino, Italo. *Italian Folktales*. New York: Harcourt Brace, 1990.

Web sites

"Christmas, New Year, and the Epiphany in Italy." [Online] http://www.notti.italiane.com/natale/welcomeb.html (accessed on January 26, 2000).

"Christmas in Italy." [Online] http://www.initaly.com/regions/xmas/xmas.htm (accessed on January 26, 2000).

Philippines

Name of Holiday: Pasko Ng Bata; Christmas; Navidad

Introduction

The Philippines is a large group of islands that lie about five hundred miles off the southeastern coast of Asia, in the western Pacific Ocean. The islands are inhabited by people who come from a variety of native ethnic backgrounds. There is also a mixture of Spanish and American influence. Because of this, Christmas is known by many different names, including Pasko Ng Bata in Pilipino, also known as Tagalog, which is the official language of the Philippines; Christmas in English, which is spoken as a second language by about half of the Filipino population; and Navidad in Spanish.

Because of the influence of early Spanish missionaries, approximately 90 percent of the population are Roman Catholic and so celebrate Christmas. The Christmas season in the Philippines is the longest in the world. It lasts twenty-two days, from December 16 through January 6, Epiphany. The people of the Philippines have combined their Spanish heritage with native island customs to create a unique Christmas celebration.

History

The first inhabitants of the Philippines were people from Indonesia and Malaya. Chinese and Muslim settlers also migrated to the islands. The Spanish began arriving in the Philippines in about 1565, and Spanish missionaries introduced the Roman Catholic religion to the native people. The Philippines were under British rule for a short time during the mid-1700s, but the Spanish reestablished their claim over the islands until 1898, when the Philippines came under U.S. control. The Philippines established an independent government, the Republic of the Philippines, in 1946.

The influence of the Spanish Roman Catholics remains strong in the Philippines. About 90 percent of modern-day Filipinos are Roman Catholic Christians, making the Philippines the only predominantly Christian country in Asia.

Filipinos have celebrated Christmas for more than four centuries. The early Spanish missionaries placed great emphasis on the Christian holidays to help attract Filipino natives to the church. The missionaries created a long Christmas season, with nine days of special dawn masses leading up to the day of Christ's birth. They also introduced special religious dramas, because the natives used this creative form in their non-Christian rituals. Catholic dramas and pageants for Christmas and Easter are still widely featured today.

Folklore, Legends, Stories

The traditional Filipino symbol of Christmas is the *parol*, a star-shaped lantern made from bamboo and paper. Two legends surround this important symbol. The first says that the parol represents the biblical bright star that guided the Three Wise Men to the manger in Bethlehem to see the Christ child. The second legend tells how the lantern was used as a light to show Mary and Joseph the way to the manger that would become Jesus' crib.

Customs, Traditions, Ceremonies

While Filipinos enjoy many of the same Christmas traditions found in countries around the world, they definitely add their own flavor. For instance, they love to decorate their homes, shops, and city streets for the Christmas season using lights, flags, candles, and Nativity scenes. They also use tropical flowers, palm fronds, and parols, the traditional Filipino bamboo lanterns.

Most Christmas activities focus on the religious aspect of the holiday and are geared toward celebrating the birth of Jesus. The Christmas season, however, is also a time for secular, or nonreligious, activities. Teens and young adults enjoy dances at night clubs, and trips to theme parks have become popular for families. Ice palaces attract large crowds to one theme park in the capital city of Manila, where the temperature is kept at a bone-chilling minus 4 degrees Fahrenheit to keep the ice from melting.

The nine *simbang-gabi*

Central to celebrating Christmas in the Philippines are the nine masses held each morning at dawn, around 4 A.M., from December 16 through December 24. In Spanish, the masses are called Misas del Gallo (pronounced MEE-sahs del GUY-oh), meaning Masses of the Cock, or Rooster. In

During a 1998 pageant, children reenact the first Christmas Eve, when Mary and Joseph sought shelter in Bethlehem so that Mary could deliver the baby Jesus. Reproduced by permission of AP/Wide World Photos.

Pilipino, these masses are called Simbang-Gabi.

Church bells call the people to morning mass, and during this nine-day religious observance leading up to Christmas Day, Filipinos display Nativity scenes called Belén, meaning "Bethlehem," in their homes and churches.

The Christmas Eve procession and mass

A Christmas Eve tradition in large Filipino communities is the Panuniuluyan (pronounced pah-noo-KNEE-oo-loo-yan),

which translates as "seeking shelter." This is a reenactment of the first Christmas Eve, when Mary and Joseph sought shelter in Bethlehem so that Mary could deliver the baby Jesus.

A woman and a man, or a boy and a girl, dress as Mary and Joseph and lead a procession through town. The procession might include carriages carrying people dressed as patron saints, hundreds of townspeople, and groups of carolers. They stop at nine different houses, knock on each door, and ask permission to stay the night. Each time the homeowner turns

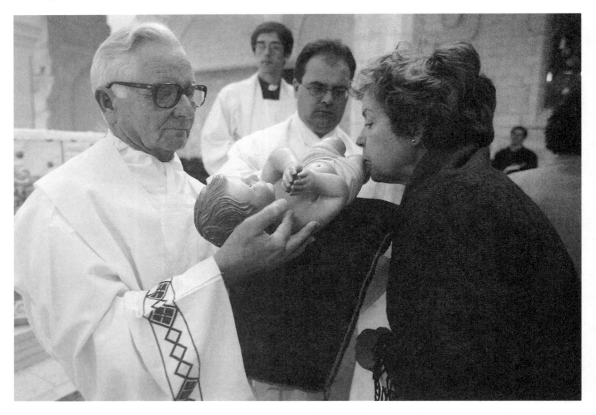

A priest holds up a doll representing the baby Jesus for worshipers to kiss at the Church of the Nativity in the city of Bethlehem in December 1999. Reproduced by permission of AP/Wide World Photos.

them away, telling them there is no room. On hearing this sad news, the carolers sing a lament (song of sorrow). When the procession reaches the church, Mary and Joseph are welcomed with singing and rejoicing, and a special mass is held to celebrate Jesus' birth.

At midnight, the church altar is unveiled to reveal a beautiful Nativity scene, with Mary and Joseph, the baby Jesus in the manger, the shepherds, and the angels. After the service, the parishioners line up to kiss the figure of the baby Jesus. Between kisses, the priest wipes the figure with a special scented cloth.

Three Kings pageants

On January 6, Epiphany, the final day of the Christmas season, cities and towns in the Philippines hold Three Kings pageants to reenact the visit of the Three Wise Men, who carried gifts to the Christ child in Bethlehem (Matthew 2:1–11). The kings are portrayed by townspeople in costume who ride through the streets on horseback looking for the Christ child in the manger. In some cities, the kings throw gifts to the crowd gathered for the pageant. In other cities, the crowd throws coins and candy to the Wise Men.

Holy Innocents' parades

At the time of the birth of Jesus, Herod was king of Judea, a region near present-day Israel that included the city of Bethlehem. According to the Bible (Matthew 2:1–16), Herod learns of the birth of Jesus from the Three Wise Men, who report that they are going to worship a new king who has just been born. Fearful that this new king will one day take the throne from him, King Herod orders his soldiers to search for the Christ child and declares that all children under age two in Bethlehem be killed. Mary and Joseph take the infant Jesus to a hiding place in Egypt until Herod's death.

Some cities in the Philippines commemorate these events on December 28, Holy Innocents' Day, with a parade. Because Herod's men did not find the baby Jesus, the parade is a happy occasion.

Masses for the Christ child

After Epiphany, churches hold ten days of special masses for the Christ child. This period is known as the fiesta season. During fiesta, people focus on the teachings of Jesus. At the end of the ten days, the people gather for the Feast of El Niño (the Holy Infant). The feast closes with a procession during which a figure of the Christ child is carried to the church.

Clothing, Costumes

During the Christmas season in the Philippines, people dress in costumes to reenact the biblical Christmas story. Children and adults may dress as Mary and Joseph, shepherds and angels, the Three Wise Men, and even King Herod and his soldiers.

December and January are cool months in the Philippines, so people dress in heavier clothing for all outdoor parades and processions. People wear their best clothes to church masses; girls often wear veils to mass.

Foods, Recipes

A favorite warm-up snack after early morning mass in the Philippines is hot ginger tea, called *salabat,* and rice cakes. Street vendors sell these treats to people on their way home from church.

After a midnight mass on Christmas Eve, many families go home to a special Christmas Eve dinner featuring dishes like delicious Filipino spring rolls, flat dough that is filled with minced vegetables and meat, rolled into an oblong cylinder, and then fried. On Christmas Day, families also serve a nice dinner, but the main feast of the season is reserved for Epiphany, January 6, the close of the holiday season.

Epiphany is the day when relatives representing every generation of a family gather for a feast of spit-roasted pig, called *lechón,* a favorite in the Philippines. It is served with garlic rice, vegetables, and beans, and lots of fresh fruit—bananas, papayas, pineapples, persimmons, and apples. The meal is capped off with numerous desserts and a cheese called *carabao,* which is made from water buffalo milk.

Arts, Crafts, Games

The chief symbol of Christmas in the Philippines is the parol, a star-shaped lantern made from bamboo and paper. The bamboo frame for the lantern is covered

Salabat (Ginger Tea)

Ingredients

1 large piece of fresh ginger root, peeled and cut into 1-inch chunks

1 medium saucepan (about 8 cups) of boiling water

1 cup (or more to taste) brown sugar or honey

Directions

1. Crush the ginger pieces with a rolling pin or kitchen mallet, then put the ginger and brown sugar or honey into the boiling water.
2. Stir to mix the sugar or honey and bring to a boil.
3. Turn heat down and simmer for 30 minutes. As water boils down, add more water to make at least 6 cups.
4. Cool and strain through a coffee filter. Serve the tea hot, with more sugar or honey if needed. Store leftover tea in the refrigerator.

with cellophane paper and then decorated with crepe paper in bright colors. An electric light bulb is placed inside to make it glow.

This decoration, called the Star of Bethlehem, takes the place of a Christmas tree in the Philippines and is displayed in every home, business, and public place during the Christmas season. Communities sometimes gather to build a large parol; competitions are held before December 16 to see which community has created the largest and prettiest lantern.

The city of San Fernando—near the Philippine capital, Manila—is a lantern-making center of the Philippines. Each December, the city holds a big lantern-display parade. Parols up to one hundred feet high are placed on trucks for the parade. They are covered with Christmas lights in many colors that flash in changing patterns to the beat of accompanying music.

Music, Dance

Caroling is a popular Christmas tradition in the Philippines. Groups of carolers are called *pastores,* shepherds, after the biblical shepherds who heard the news of Christ's birth from an angel while tending their flocks (Luke 2:8–20). Christmas carols sung in the Philippines are a combination of traditional carols brought by Spanish missionaries and Filipino folk songs. These carols are called *villancicos.*

Carolers stroll through town each evening of the Christmas season, beginning December 16. Musicians playing guitars, tambourines, and castanets accompany the singers. Caroling groups also accompany the Panuniuluyan procession on Christmas Eve and sing during masses at church.

Caroling kids

During the two weeks before Christmas, children walk through town singing Christmas carols. A favorite is "Maligayong Pasko" ("Merry Christmas"), which is sung to the tune of "Happy Birthday." The children are usually accompanied by a guitarist, and families give them money after they finish singing at each house. Children sometimes dress in costumes to go caroling, making this custom a little like Halloween trick-or-treating in Western countries.

Special Role of Children, Young Adults

In Filipino families, the elders—grandparents, godparents, and other senior family members—are considered very wise and are honored. After mass on Christmas Day and on Epiphany, parents take their children to visit their elders and exchange gifts with them. The children show their respect for grandparents and other elders by kissing their hands. Epiphany is often called "Elders' Christmas," because it is a day to honor the wisdom of older family members. After church, the whole family gathers for a big feast.

Filipino children take part in Christmas parades in some cities, wearing colorful flower wreaths and their best clothes. Children also have a big part in decorating for the Christmas season. Evergreen trees do not grow in the Philippines, so children sometimes twist green brushes or green crepe paper around other tree branches to create a make-believe Christmas tree.

Epiphany is the day when most Filipino children receive Christmas gifts, as they do in Spain, Italy, and some other European countries. The Filipino Santa Claus is sometimes depicted riding a water buffalo and wearing a headpiece made of dried fruit.

For More Information

Mendoza, Lunita. *Philippines: Festivals of the World.* Milwaukee Wis.: Gareth Stevens, 1999.

Web sites

"Christmas in the Philippines." [Online] http://christmas.com/wv/PH (accessed on February 25, 2000).

Sweden

Name of Holiday: Jul

Introduction

Swedish families observe Advent customs, which means they anticipate Christmas, called Jul (pronounced YOOL), for four weeks before it arrives on December 25. The Christmas season officially begins on December 13 with the Feast of Saint Lucia, when the oldest daughter in the family dresses in a white gown and a candlelit crown and serves special sweet buns to her family. Christmas Eve holds the biggest celebration. Parents decorate and light the Christmas tree, then children rush in to enjoy the beautiful sight. A Christmas gnome called *Jultomten* is the Swedish Santa Claus.

History

Before Christianity spread to Scandinavia (Sweden, Norway, Denmark, and Finland) during the ninth century, the Vikings and the Norsemen celebrated the winter solstice around December 21 or December 22. The solstice was a time to celebrate the renewal of the sun's cycle, when the days lengthened and the sun rose higher in the sky. The celebration was called Iol, Iul, Jule, or Yule. Yuletide means "the sun's turning."

Santa's Home in the Far North

The town of Rovaniemi, the capital of Lapland, which is part of the Scandinavian country of Finland, claims to be the real home of Santa Claus. Tourists come from all over the world—some by the Concorde, a supersonic jet—to visit Santa Claus Village, five miles outside of town, on the Arctic Circle. Santa's house is in the perfect setting, nestled among evergreens, reindeer, and snow. The village is open year-round and admission is free. A million children from 120 countries write Santa letters each Christmas; the letters are delivered by a special Finnish postal service.

The two-week celebration also honored Thor, the Norse god of thunder. During this period, all work stopped and hunting ceased. People were especially prohibited from turning wheels, because they did not want to encourage the wheel of the sun to turn faster. After the days of resting ended, a great feast was held, and a large wheel was rolled from farm to farm.

During the festival, a special beer was consumed, and a pig was probably sacrificed to the gods and then roasted for a public feast. The people believed that the amount of food prepared for the Jul feast would represent the abundance of food in the year to come.

About one thousand years ago, after Christianity had been established in north-ern Europe, Sweden's King Canute decreed that Christmas would be a one-month celebration. It started on December 13, the feast day of Saint Lucia, a Christian martyr revered by the Swedish, and lasted until January 13, Saint Canute's Day.

Folklore, Legends, Stories

Scandinavia is a region rich with folktales and known for its storytellers, including Hans Christian Andersen (1805–1875), who created such memorable Christmas stories as "The Fir Tree" and "Tinderbox," which became known as "The Little Match Girl."

Animals talking on Christmas Eve

It is an old Scandinavian belief that farm animals know when Christmas Eve arrives, and at midnight they are said to stand and bow or kneel to the Christ child from their stalls. According to folklore, they are also given the power of speech for one hour.

Rituals to keep away evil

Witches and other evil spirits were once believed to roam about after dark on Christmas Eve, and Scandinavian families performed a number of rites to prevent them from making mischief. After the floor was swept, the broom was hidden to prevent witches from riding it. Dry spruce was burned to make sparks and keep witches from coming down the chimney; salt was thrown into the fire for the same purpose.

A large candle was left burning all night, with a ring of salt around it, to ward off evil spirits. The sign of the cross was made over all the doors, and often the men and boys took their guns and walked from

The Santa Claus Village near Rovaniemi, Finland, in 1996. The lightrope marks the Arctic Circle. Reproduced by permission of AP/Wide World Photos.

farm to farm firing shots to frighten away evil spirits. This custom, called "shooting in Christmas," gave rise to today's shooting off of fireworks. Families also slept together on a large straw mat on Christmas Eve, because it was considered dangerous to sleep alone.

From the tree's point of view . . .

One of the world's best-loved Christmas stories is *The Fir Tree,* by Danish author Hans Christian Andersen. The story is about a small fir tree that is cut down to be decorated as a Christmas tree in a wealthy home. The tree enjoys splendor and admiration for a short time, then is abandoned in the loft, where it tells its story to the mice and rats. In the spring, the little tree, now withered and dry, is taken outside, chopped into pieces, and burned. But the tree had its hour of joy:

And the Fir Tree was put into a great tub filled with sand; but no one could see that it was a tub, for it was hung round with green cloth, and stood on a large, many-colored carpet. Oh, how the Tree trembled! What was to happen now? The servants and the young ladies, also, decked it out. On one branch they hung little nets cut out of colored paper—every net was filled with sweetmeats; golden apples and walnuts hung down as if they grew there;

and more than a hundred little candles, red, white, and blue, were fastened to the different boughs. Dolls that looked exactly like real people—the Tree had never seen such before—swung upon the foliage, and high on the summit of the Tree was fixed a tinsel star. It was splendid, particularly splendid. "This evening," said all, "this evening it will shine."

Customs, Traditions, Ceremonies

Advent, or "the coming" of the Christ child, celebrated for four weeks prior to Christmas, is an important part of the holiday season in both Sweden and throughout Scandinavia. Families hang up Advent calendars, light Advent candles, and display Advent wreaths, all of which originated in Scandinavia and Germany. In some apartment buildings, each family decorates a window to correspond to a day of Advent. When their day comes, a family unveils their window, lit by rows of candles, and then invites the neighbors in for refreshments.

Christmas dinner for the birds

A spirit of kindness toward animals at Christmas is especially displayed in Sweden, where every family saves the best sheaf (bundle) of grain from the fall harvest for the birds' Christmas dinner. On farms, the sheaf is placed on a pole, gateway, barn door, or rooftop or hung from a tree. In town, sheaves are purchased and left on eaves or balconies.

Farm animals are given an extra meal on Christmas Eve, the time when they are said to have watched over the infant Jesus as he lay in the manger.

Burning the Yule log

The burning of a great log during the winter solstice is an ancient custom that probably began with the Norsemen of Norway, and was carried over to the Christian celebration of Christmas in other Scandinavian and European countries, and in parts of the United States. The word "yule" is thought to derive from the Norse word *hweol*, meaning "wheel" and referring to the great wheel of the sun in its yearly cycle. Christmas is sometimes called Yuletide.

The Yule log was often a whole tree trunk or part of the root of a very large oak or ash tree. It had to be large enough to burn for the twelve days of Christmas and still have a small piece left over with which to kindle the following year's log. An old Norse belief was that each spark from the Yule log represented a new chicken, pig, lamb, goat, or calf to be born in the coming year.

Besides bringing light and warmth to the cold, dark days of winter, the Yule log was believed to drive off evil spirits that might be lurking. The great Yule fire was also believed to burn away hard feelings and wrongs between people and end feuds between families.

After the Christmas season, the remaining portion of the log was kept under a bed or in another safe place until the following Christmas. Ashes from the Yule fire were believed to have magic properties, such as the power to cure illness, protect homes from storms and lightning, and ensure a year of good crops.

Today, any large log burned during the Christmas season may be considered a Yule log. The Yule candle, a large candle burned on each night of the twelve days of

Christmas, was a companion to the Yule log in Scandinavia and northern Europe.

Dipping in the kettle

Swedes have a Christmas Eve custom called "dipping in the kettle," which reenacts a time of famine when people lived on only broth and bread. A broth made of sausages, pork, and other meats is prepared in a large kettle, and everyone in the family dips a piece of bread into the broth and eats it. Afterward, Christmas Eve dinner is served.

Lighting the tree

Decorating the Christmas tree was a custom introduced from Germany into Scandinavia during the nineteenth century. On Christmas Eve, parents in Swedish families decorate the Christmas tree behind closed doors as a surprise for the children. Decorations are usually simple; the most popular are straw goats and pigs. Other tree decorations are gnomes, birds, pine cones, cotton "snow" and glitter "frost," candy, and paper flags of many countries. The tree is also decorated with many lights, or sometimes candles.

Most families have a traditional homemade Nativity, or manger, scene that is placed near the tree. Gifts brought by the Swedish "Santa," Jultomten (pronounced yool-TOM-ten), are placed beneath the Christmas tree. When the parents finish decorating the tree, the doors are opened and the children are allowed to come in.

Jultomten, the Christmas gnome

In Sweden, children believe that Jultomten, a little old gnome with a long white beard and a red suit with a winter cap, brings presents on Christmas Eve, just as Santa Claus does in the United States.

But unlike the rotund Santa, Jultomten is a skinny little man who looks like an Irish leprechaun or a mischievous elf.

Swedish folklore says that gnomes are present in every household, and each house is protected by its own *tomten,* or gnome, who lives in the attic. On Christmas Eve, children put out for the household gnome a bowlful of special Christmas rice pudding, called *Jul-gröt,* that has a lump of butter in the center.

In many families, the father dresses up as Jultomten and comes knocking at the door on Christmas Eve, bringing a sackful of gifts for the children. Before leaving he might ask, "Are there any good children in this house?" Of course, on Christmas Eve, all the children are good.

Christmas rhyming

When Swedes give gifts at Christmas, each gift bears an original poem or rhyme written by the giver. Each rhyme is read aloud as the gift is given. The rhymes may be about things that happened during the year, about secret wishes, or any number of humorous subjects. This tradition comes from an old custom called "Christmas knocks." A person would silently approach a neighbor's door, knock hard, and when the door was opened, throw a present inside and run away before he could be recognized. The gift would have a teasing rhyme written on the wrapping. Even today, Jul gifts are called *julklapp* (pronounced YOOL-klap), or "Christmas knocks."

A quiet Christmas Day

On Christmas Day, people in Sweden observe Christ's birth by going to church. The first service is held at about 7 A.M. and is called Julottan (pronounced yool-OT-tun). Candles are lit in both homes and churches. It is a quiet day filled with beauty and light. On December 26, called Second Day Christmas, the holiday fun begins anew and continues until Saint Canute's Day, January 13.

Foods, Recipes

The traditional Christmas meal, which is eaten on Christmas Eve, begins with foods arranged on the bountiful Swedish *smörgåsbord* (pronounced SMOR-gus-bord). Such foods include pickled herring, smoked sausage, ham, red cabbage, fried meatballs, and Swedish salads. Following the smorgasbord is the *lutfisk,* a traditionally prepared saltwater fish, with a special creamy sauce. Many different types of pastries end the feast.

Swedish *Jul-gröt* and the lucky almond

The main dish for Christmas Eve dinner in Sweden and other Scandinavian countries is a boiled rice pudding called *Jul-gröt* (pronounced YOOL-grot) or *risengrød* (pronounced RYE-sen-grod). It is flavored with cinnamon and powdered sugar and has a pool of melted butter in the center and a ring of honey around the outside. Hidden inside the pudding is one almond. According to folklore, the person who gets the almond, if single, will be married within the year. In Denmark, the person who finds the almond simply gets a piece of marzipan, an almond sweet.

Music, Dance

In Sweden, after the gifts are opened the Christmas Eve ceremonies end with the *judgedance,* a circle dance around the tree. Everyone circles counterclockwise except one person, who circles clockwise inside the circle while holding a lighted candle. They sing a traditional song:

Now 'tis Yuletide again!
Yuletide will last till Easter.
No, this can't be so,
For between the two
Comes Lent.

When the song stops, the person holding the candle stops in front of a person in the circle. If that person cannot help but smile, he or she takes a turn in the center with the candle.

Special Role of Children, Young Adults

The Christmas season begins on December 13 in Sweden with the Feast of Saint Lucia (pronounced loo-SEE-ah), who is also known as the Queen of Light. Saint Lucia was a fourth-century Christian saint from Sicily who was punished for her religious beliefs. Although little is known of her life, some accounts say she lost her sight while being tortured or that she blinded herself to protest the cruel treatment of Christians. She is known as the patron saint of the blind.

Saint Lucia is said to have appeared to the Swedish people during a famine in the Middle Ages (about 500–1500). According to legend, she wore a crown of fire. Soon after her appearance, ships came with loads of grain for the starving people. She has since been a symbol of hope and plentiful harvests. Her festival is celebrated with the lighting of many candles.

It is the custom for the oldest daughter in the household to wake up first on Saint

Swedish Christmas Bowknots

Ingredients

4 egg yolks

2 tablespoons butter or margarine, melted

1 teaspoon vanilla extract

grated rind of 1 lemon

about ¼ cup of powdered sugar

1¼ cups all-purpose flour

vegetable oil

Directions

1. Mix together egg yolks and powdered sugar until thick and fluffy, about 3 minutes.
2. Add vanilla, melted butter or margarine, and lemon rind. Mix well.
3. Add flour a little at a time and mix with your hands to form a ball of smooth dough. Cover the bowl and refrigerate for 1 hour.
4. Roll out dough with a floured rolling pin on a floured work surface. Keep rolling until it is very thin, about ⅛-inch thick.
5. Cut dough into 8-inch-long strips, about ¾-inch wide.
6. With a knife, make a 1-inch slit, lengthwise, about 2 inches from the end of each strip. Form a loop from the dough by slipping the end opposite the cut through the slit and pulling gently.
7. Keep the bowknots from drying out by covering them with a damp towel until all the dough is used.
8. With adult help, heat the oil in a deep fryer to 375 degrees.
9. Gently lower the bowknots into the hot oil a few at a time and fry for about 3 minutes. They should be golden brown.
10. When done, remove with a slotted spoon and drain on paper towels. Sprinkle with powdered sugar while still warm.

Makes about 2 dozen bowknots

Lucia's Day. She dresses in a long white gown with a red sash, and puts on a crown of winter greenery with either seven or nine lighted candles. She then acts out the traditional role of the Lucia bride, or Lussibruden.

The girl goes into her parents' bedroom and to each bedroom in the house, singing a song to awaken her family. She also serves them a hot drink and special buns called *lussekatter* (pronounced LOO-sa-katter; Lucia cats), which are believed to ward off evil spirits and bring good luck. When everyone is up, breakfast is served in a room full of lighted candles. Even the animals of the house get a special portion.

Beginning on Saint Lucia's Day, the family works together to do the Christmas baking and prepare for the month-long Christmas celebration. Saint Lucia's Day is sometimes called Lilla Jul (Little Yule) because it is the beginning of the Christmas season. Some towns in Sweden and other Scandinavian countries hold Saint Lucia's Day beauty contests and parades by torchlight.

For More Information

McNair, Sylvia. *Sweden: Enchantment of the World.* Chicago, Ill.: Children's Press, 1998.

Rabe, Monica. *Sweden: Festivals of the World.* Milwaukee, Wis.: Gareth Stevens, 1998.

Web sites

"Christmas in Sweden." [Online] http://www.swedenemb.org/xmas.html (accessed on January 27, 2000).

"Lucia's Day in Sweden." [Online] http://www.best.com/~swanson/holidays/nora.html (accessed on January 27, 2000).

United States

Name of Holiday: Christmas; Yule; Noel; Feast of the Nativity

Introduction

Christmas is arguably the best-loved and most widely celebrated holiday in the United States. Immigrants from many lands brought their customs to the United States, where they combined to form the American Christmas. Many families still prepare ethnic foods and follow Christmas customs that recall their heritage. Other traditions, including the Santa Claus legend and the community Christmas tree, are uniquely American.

History

In 1607, English settlers founded Jamestown, Virginia, the first permanent settlement in America. In spite of the hardships of the new land, they celebrated Christmas as they had done in England, with warm fires and plenty to eat for their Christmas feast.

Members of a religious group called the Puritans, who emigrated from England to the Plymouth and Massachusetts Bay colonies in the 1620s, did not believe in celebrating Christmas, however. They believed the Bible commanded people to rest from work only one day a week, on Sunday, and that Christmas celebrations were too much like the pagan holidays of the Romans. The celebration of Christmas was outlawed by the General Court of Massachusetts Bay from 1659 to 1681.

During the 1600s and 1700s, settlers continued to arrive in America from many different lands, bringing their varied religious beliefs and their Old World Christmas customs with them. For many years, these communities celebrated Christmas in the ways of their homeland. Eventually the customs blended together into an American celebration that took in the most popular nonreligious traditions while allowing each religious group to worship in its own way.

To those who were not particularly religious, Christmas and New Year's was a time for eating and drinking too much, playing games, gambling, shooting guns and fireworks, and mumming—dressing in disguises and going from house to house asking for food, drink, or money. In the South, plantation owners gave slaves the day off and shared holiday food and drinks with them. Some owners also gave them money or clothing in a Christmas box, following the English custom of Boxing Day. On Boxing Day it was traditional to give gifts to servants and public workers.

The states unite on Christmas

After the American Revolution (1775–83), the newly formed thirteen colonies wanted to break from English traditions. As part of this movement, English holiday dates were removed from the American calendar. Only a few special days, including Thanksgiving and New Year's, were celebrated during the year.

About fifty years later, however, as the United States grew in commerce, transportation, industry, and communications, and as its cities developed, people wished for a return to old-fashioned holiday celebrations. New York author Washington Irving (1783–1859) did much to re-create the old Dutch and English Christmas customs through his books, especially *A History of New York* (1809) and *The Sketchbook of Geoffrey Crayon, Gent* (1819–20).

As Catholic, Lutheran, Episcopalian, and Baptist churches began to hold special Christmas services, other churches moved toward observing the holiday. In 1823, American professor Clement C. Moore's poem "A Visit from St. Nicholas," often called "The Night Before Christmas," introduced Santa Claus and his reindeer as they are still known and loved today. By 1830, New York City was celebrating

Christmas Is Recognized in the New World

Christopher Columbus (1451–1506), the Spanish explorer who is credited with discovering the New World, sailed west from Spain in the fall of the year 1492. In December, one of his three ships, the *Santa María,* ran aground on what is now the island of Haiti. The island natives helped Columbus and his men and prepared a feast. The Spaniards built a fort from the abandoned ship's timber and called the fort *La Navidad,* or the Nativity.

Christmas in full swing; stores stayed open late for Christmas shoppers, and Christmas decorations became popular.

Alabama, Louisiana, and Arkansas were the first states to make Christmas a legal holiday, in 1836, 1837, and 1838. Other states quickly followed, and, in 1870, Christmas was declared a federal holiday in the United States.

The family, the tree, and Christmas today

Even though the drinking and rowdiness of Christmas and New Year's continued in most of the nation, during the 1800s the country was also influenced by Great Britain's Queen Victoria (1819–1901) and Prince Albert (1819–1861). In 1841, Prince Albert, who was originally from Germany, brought the German tradition of the Christmas tree to Windsor Castle, the home he shared with Queen Victoria and their children. News of the family celebrations spread and caused more people to think of Christmas as a family holiday—a time to decorate Christmas trees, give gifts, and share holiday feasts.

Victorian-era England also gave North America and Europe many ideas for Christmas decorating. Today, Americans still decorate with velvet ribbons trimmed in gold, spread lace tablecloths on holiday tables, and string berries to trim the tree. By 1900, the Christmas tree had become an American tradition, with one American household in five decorating a tree. Many people held on to the old Dutch custom of hanging Christmas stockings instead of—or in addition to—putting up a tree.

During the American Civil War (1861–65), people held on to the new Christmas traditions—they became even more important because so many families could not be together. Soldiers did their best to celebrate in whatever way they could on the battlefields. In 1863, New York artist Thomas Nast, who worked for *Harper's* magazine, drew pictures of Santa Claus visiting Union (Northern) troops.

During the 1860s to 1880s, Boston printer Louis Prang developed the first successful Christmas card business, and sending cards became a new American tradition.

By the 1900s, the "melting pot" of cultures that make up the United States had combined Christmas customs from many lands. In many families, however, special ethnic recipes and customs handed down from generations past have remained a part of the Christmas celebration.

Folklore, Legends, Stories

When people from all countries came to live in the United States, they brought with them their stories and superstitions along with their traditions and customs. Some of these tales are still remembered; others have changed over time to become uniquely American.

Christmas superstitions

Many superstitions about the Christmas season were brought to America by early settlers from Europe. People believed that weather could be predicted for the new year by the weather on Christmas Day. Wearing new clothes on Christmas Day was believed to bring good luck during the new year, but if one wore new shoes it would bring catastrophe. It was considered bad luck to let a fire go out on Christmas morning. Eating an apple at midnight on Christmas Eve would bring a healthy year, and leaving a loaf of bread on the table after supper would mean plenty of food. If someone fixed a roof between Christmas and New Year's, the patches would fail and the holes come back.

The Santa Claus legend

The most popular American Christmas legend is that of Santa Claus, who is said to live at the North Pole with his wife, Mrs. Claus. Santa works in his shop—with the help of his elves—year-round to make toys for good boys and girls. Then, on Christmas Eve, he packs all the toys in a huge sack and throws it on his sleigh, which is pulled by a faithful team of reindeer, and flies through the air to deliver the toys. At each stop, Santa lands his sleigh on the rooftop, slides down the chimney with his sack, and places the toys under the

Christmas tree. By Christmas morning, Santa has magically delivered gifts to children all over the world.

The Santa legend was originally brought to America from Dutch and English immigrants in the 1700s. He was known as Saint Nicholas, or Sinterklaas, a fourth-century bishop known for his kindness and generosity. Throughout the 1800s and into the 1900s, Sinterklaas evolved, helped along by American authors, artists, and advertising writers, into the image that is known today.

A creation of pen and ink: Many of the creators of Santa Claus lived in the growing city of New York, originally settled by the Dutch. American author Washington Irving, a member of the New York Historical Society, was among the first to describe Saint Nicholas, in *Knickerbocker's History of New York*, published on Saint Nicholas Day in 1809:

> And lo, the good Saint Nicholas came riding over the tops of the trees, in that self-same wagon wherein he brings his yearly presents to children ... and as he smoked the smoke from his pipe ascended into the air and spread like a cloud overhead.... And when Saint Nicholas had smoked his pipe, he twisted it in his hatband, and laying his finger beside his nose, gave the astonished Van Kortlandt a very significant look, then mounting his wagon he returned over the tree-tops and disappeared.

In 1822, Clement Clarke Moore, a professor who lived in New York City, wrote a poem called "A Visit from St. Nicholas" for his children, never intending to have it published. A friend read it, however, and then sent it to the New York *Troy Sentinel*. The *Sentinel* published the poem on December 23, 1823, and reprinted it each year at Christmastime. Other newspapers printed the poem as well. It was finally published in the *New York Book of Poetry* in 1837, eventually to become one of the most popular poems in America's history.

As Moore's poem was printed and reprinted throughout the United States, his vision of Santa Claus and his reindeer became the American vision. Artists began drawing pictures of Santa and his visits, and a Christmas symbol was born that remains to this day.

One well-known artist responsible for creating the image of Santa was New York cartoonist Thomas Nast. Nast worked for the magazine *Harper's Weekly,* where for thirty years he drew seasonal illustrations of Santa Claus and created Santa's world as children still know it today. He completed his first illustration of Moore's poem in 1863. In 1881, he drew a portrait of Santa Claus as a round-bellied, white-haired, bearded little man with a red coat trimmed in white fur who smoked a long pipe. As interest in the North Pole grew during the middle 1800s, Nast chose this location for Santa's home.

The Santa image we have today comes mostly from drawings done from 1931 to 1964 by an artist named Haddon Sundblom. Sundblom created his Santas for Coca-Cola advertisements that appeared on the back covers of *Post* and *National Geographic* magazines.

Rudolph, the Red-Nosed Reindeer

A Christmas story that has become as much a part of the Santa Claus legend as Santa himself is "Rudolph, the Red-Nosed Reindeer," written in 1939 by Robert L. May, an employee of Montgomery Ward

Yes, Virginia, There Is a Santa Claus

Belief in Santa Claus is encouraged by parents, who make every effort to make him real to their children. They answer children's letters to Santa, stay up on Christmas Eve putting gifts under the tree after the children have gone to bed, eat cookies and drink milk left for Santa, and even dress in Santa Claus costumes themselves to keep young children believing.

When eight-year-old Virginia O'Hanlon of New York City wrote to the New York *Sun* in 1897 for the truth about Santa after her friends expressed doubt, editorial writer Francis Church set the record straight once and for all:

Yes, Virginia, there is a Santa Claus. He exists as certainly as love, and generosity and devotion exist, and you know that they abound and give to your life its highest beauty and joy. Alas! How dreary would be the world if there were no Santa Claus! It would be as dreary as if there were no Virginias....

Nobody sees Santa Claus, but that is no sign that there is no Santa Claus. The most real things in the world are those that neither children nor men can see....

No Santa Claus! Thank God! he lives and lives forever. A thousand years from now, Virginia, nay, ten times ten thousand years from now, he will continue to make glad the heart of childhood.

department stores. More than two million copies of the story-poem were given to the children of the stores' customers that year. It became so popular that another 3.5 million copies were distributed in 1946.

In 1947, the story was published and sold 100,000 copies. In 1949, the song "Rudolph, the Red-Nosed Reindeer" was written by Johnny Marks and recorded by singer Gene Autry. It soon became a Christmas classic. The story of Rudolph was translated into some twenty-five languages and was produced as a television show, which is viewed by millions each Christmas.

Rudolph is a young reindeer who is made fun of by all the other reindeer because he has a big red shiny nose. But then, on a foggy Christmas Eve, Santa's reindeer are having trouble navigating the sleigh because they cannot see. Santa remembers how Rudolph's red nose glows and calls on him to guide the reindeer team through the fog. Rudolph saves Christmas for all the girls and boys and becomes a hero.

Christmas from American pens

American authors and poets have written about Christmas for more than a century. Some of the more famous short stories are "A Merry Christmas," from *Little Women* (1868), by Louisa May Alcott (1832–1888); "Christmas in the Big Woods," from *Little House in the Big Woods* (1932), by Laura Ingalls Wilder (1867–1957); "The Gift of the Magi," by O. Henry (real name William Sydney Porter; 1862–1910); "The Christmas of the Phonograph Records"

(1966), by Mari Sandoz (1896–1966); and *A Christmas Memory* (1966), by Truman Capote (1924–1984).

Among the best-loved Christmas poems by Americans are "The Bells," by Edgar Allan Poe (1809–1849); "Christmas Morning," by Elizabeth Madox Roberts (1886–1941); "Christmas Trees," by Robert Frost (1874–1963); and "Carol of the Brown King," by Langston Hughes (1902–1967).

Hundreds of other Christmas stories, poems, children's books, and films for television and motion pictures have been created by Americans. Two of the most popular are *How the Grinch Stole Christmas* (book, 1957; teleplay, 1966), by Dr. Seuss (real name Theodor Geisel; 1904–1991), and *A Charlie Brown Christmas* (teleplay 1966), by cartoonist Charles M. Schulz (1922–2000).

Customs, Traditions, Ceremonies

Ask Americans about Christmas traditions and they will probably tell you about the traditions in their own families. But a few basic ways of keeping Christmas are common to most Americans. Christmas in the United States usually means decorating a Christmas tree and doing a lot of shopping in the weeks before Christmas to buy gifts for family members and friends. It also means sending Christmas cards or writing Christmas letters; baking cookies, cakes, and pies; and cleaning the house from top to bottom to get ready for guests. Many people hang an evergreen wreath on the front door, put candles in the windows, and decorate the house with colored lights.

Young children look forward to a Christmas Eve visit from Santa Claus. They may write letters to Santa telling him what they would like for Christmas or have their pictures taken with him in a department store, while whispering their wishes in his ear as they sit on his knee. On Christmas Eve, many children hang up Christmas stockings to receive small gifts, candy, and fruit on Christmas morning. Some children put milk and cookies under the tree for Santa.

Catholic families attend midnight mass on Christmas Eve. Many other churches have candlelight services or special church services on Christmas Eve and Christmas Day. Some families open gifts on Christmas Eve and some on the morning of Christmas Day.

During the afternoon of Christmas Day, family and friends gather for a special dinner and give thanks for another Christmas together. Family members who live in different towns or states try to come together at Christmas, often gathering at the home of their parents. Returning home for Christmas is a tradition in the United States and worldwide.

Bonfires, candles, and billions of lights

A big part of the American Christmas tradition is displaying lights. From the luminarias (pronounced loo-mi-NAIR-ee-uhs) of Hispanic American communities all over the Southwest to the Christmas bonfires along the Mississippi River in Louisiana to the dazzling lights on the gigantic tree at Rockefeller Center in New York City—the United States glows during the Christmas season.

A luminaria, or "little light," is a small, lighted candle placed inside a little paper bag left open at the top, with sand or gravel in the bottom to hold it upright.

A giant saguaro cactus lights up the desert in Chandler, Arizona, in 1997. Whether the scenery includes snow or sandy beaches, anyone who is in the United States during December will know it is Christmas because of the lights. Reproduced by permission of AP/Wide World Photos.

A century-old tradition in southern Louisiana is to light Christmas Eve bonfires along the Mississippi River levee. People pick a spot for their family bonfire and, beginning around the first of November, gather just about anything that will burn—including old rubber tires, scrap wood, dry willow branches, and cardboard. To make a bigger fire that will last longer, some create tepees or pyramids of the materials; others build mock houses and burnable sculptures.

Bonfires were built on New Year's Eve for many years, but in 1884, store owner George Bourgeois built the first Christmas Eve bonfire on the levee to burn empty boxes. Riverboats stopped to see what was causing the fire, and boatmen found themselves joining Bourgeois in a Christmas Eve celebration, playing poker and eating gumbo, a spicy seafood and vegetable stew. A few years later, fathers and sons began building their own bonfires on Christmas Eve. Today, the tradition draws crowds from miles around. The bonfires are at the center of big festivals, which often include free concerts and gumbo dinners after a midnight mass.

Luminarias are arranged along sidewalks and driveways or paths, traditionally to light the way for Mary and Joseph and the Christ child. The tradition was introduced to Mexico by the Spaniards during the 1500s. The first luminarias were small bonfires or paper lanterns hung from trees. Today, communities throughout the United States decorate with luminarias at Christmas, usually on one special night during the holiday season.

Whether the scenery includes snow and icicles or palm trees and sandy beaches, anyone who is in the United States during December will know it is Christmas because of the lights. Christmas lights adorn every Christmas tree, many homes and lawns, most stores, streets, skyscrapers, bridges, and parks. Candles glow inside churches and shops, mark the Sundays in Advent, and draw Christmas carolers to homes. The billions of lights that turn ordinary scenes into fairy tales are very much a part of the magic of Christmas.

A favorite activity when families get together at Christmas is to walk or drive around neighborhoods to see how other families have decorated. Some displays are so spectacular they take weeks to arrange. New attractions at theme parks include special Christmas characters and scenes created entirely with lights. Some organizations stage elaborate light displays and raise money for charities by charging admission.

Even in Barrow, Alaska, the northernmost part of the United States—where the sun never shines on Christmas Day—colored lights decorate igloos (homes made of ice and snow) and arches built of whale jawbones to help families celebrate the season.

The community Christmas tree

During the early 1700s, German immigrants to America were among the first to decorate Christmas trees in the United States. A treasured custom in Germany, the Christmas tree became more popular in the United States as the number of German immigrants increased during the early to middle 1800s.

After Christmas trees were made popular in England during the 1840s by Queen Victoria and Prince Albert, the custom spread even more throughout the United States. It became especially popular in New York, where the first Christmas tree merchant began selling trees from the Catskill Mountains in 1851. The popular ladies' magazine *Godey's Lady's Book* featured article after article on Christmas trees—telling its readers how large the tree should be and making suggestions on how to decorate it.

In 1856, President Franklin Pierce (1804–1869) put the first Christmas tree in the White House, and by the late 1800s, the White House Christmas tree had become an American tradition. In 1923, President Calvin Coolidge (1872–1933) was the first president to light the newly planted National Living Christmas Tree on the White House grounds. The lighting of this national tree is now an annual event.

An American tradition known throughout the world is the magnificent Christmas light display at Rockefeller Center in New York City. The first giant Christmas tree was put up at Rockefeller Center in 1933, in hopes of raising the spirits of Americans suffering through the Great Depression, a time of widespread unemployment and poverty in the United States. The first tree at Rockefeller Center was not as tall as the seventy- to ninety-foot trees of today, and it had only seven hundred lights as opposed to the thousands of lights that now adorn the trees.

The Christmas tree traditions at the White House and Rockefeller Center heralded a custom that is said to be truly American: decorating a community Christmas tree. Other cities and towns began to decorate a tree in prominent public settings, such as town squares or parks, the front lawns of public buildings, or at major traffic intersections. Today, probably every municipality, from the smallest community to the largest city, has its own Christmas tree. A Christmas parade on or shortly after Thanksgiving, along with the lighting of the town tree, begins the Christmas season.

Helping others: A Christmas tradition

Americans firmly believe that Christmas should be a happy time for everyone, if possible. For this reason, giving to charity has become a part of the American Christmas tradition, as it is in many other countries. Volunteers for the charitable orga-

More than five hundred tuba players participate in the Annual Tuba Christmas Concert at the Rockefeller Center skating rink in New York City in 1997. The first giant Christmas tree was put up at Rockefeller Center in 1933. Reproduced by permission of AP/Wide World Photos.

nization the Salvation Army dress in Santa Claus suits and ring bells on the streets during the Christmas season; shoppers drop change and dollar bills into their collection buckets to help the poor. Chambers of commerce, police and fire departments, and other organizations hold Christmas toy drives to make sure that every child in the community receives at least one gift. People make extra donations to organizations that fight illness and seek cures for disease.

Adults and children may spend a weekend or even Christmas Eve working to feed the homeless in soup kitchens. Children go caroling to bring cheer to those in nursing homes. Merchants collect canned goods for food pantries that feed the hungry, and people who know someone who might be alone on Christmas make a special point of visiting that person on Christmas Eve or Christmas Day.

Foods, Recipes

Turkey and cranberry sauce are uniquely American foods that have been a

Thanksgiving and Christmas dinner tradition since American Indians introduced these foods to the Pilgrims during the 1600s. The main dish for a traditional American Christmas dinner is often roast turkey with a stuffing made from bread crumbs and seasoning, and sometimes including apples, sausage, or other special ingredients, depending on the region and the cook. Cranberry sauce accompanies the turkey. Ham and the traditional English roast goose or roast duck are other popular main dishes

The main dish is served with mashed potatoes and gravy and side dishes like yams, corn, peas, beans, deviled eggs, potato salad, pickles, and breads. Pumpkin, mincemeat, pecan, apple, and cherry pies as well as plum pudding, cakes, and cookies are typical desserts. Hot apple cider, eggnog, fruit punch, wine, coffee, tea, and hot chocolate are popular beverages. Eggnog is a sweet drink made with eggs, milk, and spices such as cinnamon, nutmeg, and cloves. Sometimes, it can also be mixed with alcoholic beverages, such as rum or brandy.

Of course, families may continue to prepare the traditional dishes of other countries, handed down from grandmothers and great-grandmothers. For example, people of Polish ancestry may serve Polish sausage and poppyseed cake, and people of French ancestry may serve the traditional oysters and, for dessert, the rich *bûche de Noël* (pronounced BOOSH duh no-EL), a cake made to look like a Yule log.

Arts, Crafts, Games

Some of the most well-known American Christmas art includes the Santa Claus drawings of Thomas Nast and of Had-don Sundblom—who drew the familiar Coca-Cola Santa Claus advertisements that appeared in advertising from 1931 to 1964—and the Christmas cards created by Louis Prang and his artists.

Because the United States is such a "melting pot" of cultures, Christmas arts

Christmas Cranberry Bread

Ingredients
2 cups flour
½ teaspoon salt
½ teaspoon baking soda
1½ teaspoons baking powder
1 cup sugar
¾ cup orange juice
1 cup fresh, chopped cranberries
1 egg
1 stick butter, softened
1 tablespoon grated orange rind
½ cup chopped nuts (almonds, pecans, or walnuts)

Directions
1. Cream together butter and sugar, then add egg, mixing well. Slowly add orange juice and orange rind.
2. Sift together flour, salt, soda, and baking powder. Add to butter mixture and fold in chopped cranberries and nuts.
3. Pour mixture into a greased, floured bread loaf pan and bake at 350 degrees for 1 hour.

Skiers glide down a mountain during the annual Christmas Eve Torchlight Parade in Winter Park, Colorado, in 1995. Reproduced by permission of AP/Wide World Photos.

ping paper in red, gold, green, and white, snow and icicles, and glitter and bows are part of a typical American Christmas.

Many Americans love to shop for a few new Christmas tree ornaments each year, and families often collect them over time. Special Christmas stores offer Christmas scenes, ornaments, and decorations year round. Some cities and towns have Christmas markets similar to those in European and Latin American countries. Both adults and children love to try their hand at making Christmas stockings, cards, and table decorations. As the Internet has grown in popularity during the last few years, many American artisans are selling their Christmas wares from their own World Wide Web sites.

Music, Dance

Christmas carols were first written in Europe during the 1300s; the practice quickly spread throughout Europe in the centuries that followed. When English, French, and German immigrants came to America, they brought the tradition with them.

A few famous carols written by Americans are "It Came Upon the Midnight Clear" (late 1800s), by Edmund H. Sears, a Massachusetts minister, with music by Richard S. Will; "O Little Town of Bethlehem" (1865), by Phillips Brooks, a Boston minister, with music by Louis H. Redner; and "We Three Kings of Orient Are" (1857), by an Episcopalian minister, John Henry Hopkins Jr. The lively Christmas song "Jingle Bells" (1856) was also written during the nineteenth century—by John Pierpont, a Unitarian minister from Boston.

and crafts can take many forms. Some people prefer to decorate with an old-fashioned style popular in Victorian England (middle to late 1800s), using flowers, ribbons, lace, and wreaths made from evergreens and holly. Families of northern or eastern European heritage might prefer handpainted Christmas tree ornaments, embroidered tablecloths, and hand-carved Santa figures. Those of Hispanic descent might create their own Nativity scenes and decorate with luminarias. Whatever the cultural background, Christmas trees, Santa Claus, wrap-

Bethlehem, Pennsylvania

On the afternoon of Christmas Eve, December 24, the Moravian church in Bethlehem, Pennsylvania—which is known as America's Christmas City—holds a special service just for children. It is called the Moravian Love Feast. The children sit together in the front of the church and sing hymns. They are then served warm, sweet buns and hot, sweet coffee. Afterward, each child is given a lighted, handmade, beeswax candle, which he or she holds for the remainder of the church service. A paper ruffle at the base prevents hot wax from dripping on the children's hands.

On Christmas Eve, the church holds a similar service for the congregation, called the Christmas Eve Vigil. The church is dark except for a bright star hanging from the ceiling, and a soft light over a picture of the Holy Family (Mary, Joseph, and the Christ child). The service consists of nearly all music; the children usually sing at least one hymn. A child from the Sunday School leads the other children in singing everyone's favorite Christmas hymn:

> Morning Star, O cheering sight!
> Ere Thou cam'st how dark earth's night!
> Jesus mine, In me shine;
> Fill my heart with light divine.

At the end of the service, everyone in the church is given a candle, which not only brings light into the dark church, but symbolizes bringing warmth into every heart.

The Moravians are named for a region called Moravia, which is now part of the Czech Republic, in eastern Europe. The Moravian missionaries who settled Bethlehem, Pennsylvania, immigrated to America from Germany in the middle 1700s. The Moravian church in Old Salem, North Carolina, holds Christmas services similar to those in Bethlehem.

Popular Christmas songs

During the twentieth century, Christmas and its modern-day legends became the subject of dozens of popular songs, such as "White Christmas," written by American composer Irving Berlin and featured in the 1942 movie *Holiday Inn;* "The Christmas Song (Chestnuts Roasting on an Open Fire)" (1946), with words by Mel Torme, lyrics by Robert Wells; "Winter Wonderland" (1934), by Felix Bernard and Richard B. Smith; and "Santa Claus Is Coming to Town" (1934), by Haven Gillespie and J. Fred Coots.

Special Role of Children, Young Adults

Since the late 1800s, Christmas has been considered a time especially for children. In the United States that means many children receive toys and gifts they have asked for at Christmas, as well as a few surprises. They also participate in a number of Christmas activities. In addition to visiting Santa Claus in department stores and shopping malls, they join in Christmas parades, and are featured in pageants and plays held in churches and schools. Church pageants are based on the Christmas story from the Bible, and children play the roles of Mary and Joseph, the angels, the shepherds, and the Three Wise Men. At school, Christmas plays usually have a secular, or nonreligious, theme, and feature characters like Santa Claus, Rudolph, elves, and fairies.

Children help make Christmas decorations for their classrooms, sing Christmas carols, and are treated to Christmas parties before school is out for a two-week holiday break. Christmas vacation is a time when families often travel to visit relatives. Children help with Christmas baking, shopping, gift wrapping, and decorating. They may also volunteer with their parents or a school or church group that visits the elderly, feeds the hungry, or takes gifts to less fortunate children.

For More Information

Christmas in Colonial and Early America. Chicago, Ill.: World Book, 1997.

Harrison, Jim. *American Christmas.* Marietta, Ga.: Longstreet Press, 1994.

Miles, Clement A. *Christmas Customs and Traditions.* New York: Dover Publications, 1989.

Web sites
"Christmas in the United States." [Online] http://christmas.com/wv/US (accessed on February 25, 2000).

Venezuela
Name of Holiday: Navidad

Introduction

The Spanish Roman Catholic influence in Venezuela, as in most South American countries, can be seen in its Christmas celebrations. Christmas or Navidad (pronounced nah-vee-DAHD; Nativity) festivities center around homemade Nativity scenes called *pesebres,* and attending Christmas mass is the highlight of the season. Children are especially anxious to see Christmas come, so they can participate in activities like roller skating to mass and reciting poems to the Christ child figure at *paradura* parties.

History

The Spanish began to colonize the South American country of Venezuela in 1521. They introduced Spanish customs, the Spanish language, and their religion—Roman Catholicism. Among the first Spanish colonists were Dominican and Franciscan priests, who came to raise cattle and to develop coffee, cocoa, and sugar plantations.

By the mid-1700s, Roman Catholicism had reached even remote areas of Venezuela, and many beautiful Catholic churches had been built. The churches were primarily responsible for the education and cultural development of the people, both native and European.

Many of the native Indian peoples, the Arawak, Cariban, and Chibcha, were made slaves to work on the Spanish sugar and coffee plantations. Through contact with their European conquerors, they contracted diseases such as smallpox; many of them died. When the natives died, the Spanish brought African slaves from the nearby Caribbean islands to work on the plantations.

The large percentage of African peoples added their cultural influence to that of the Indians and the Europeans. German and Portuguese colonists also influenced Venezuela, Brazil, Colombia, and other South American countries.

Today, about 97 percent of Venezuelans are Roman Catholic, and their Christmas customs, like those of most of Latin America, have kept their Spanish flavor. In addition to Spanish ways of celebrating—including making Nativity scenes and attending midnight mass on Christmas Eve—Venezuelans have added foods, music, and customs of the Caribbean, African, and native Indian peoples who make up the population. One of these is the extremely popular *Gaita* music, a combination of Spanish and African rhythms heard everywhere during the Christmas season.

With the discovery of oil in Venezuela in 1910, the nation became more prosperous, and, like much of South America, has been influenced by North American culture. Since about 1950, Christmas trees have become more and more popular in Venezuela, Colombia, Argentina, Brazil, and other Latin American countries, sometimes replacing the Nativity scenes commonly constructed in homes at Christmas.

Although many children still receive gifts from the Three Kings on the eve of Epiphany, many today also get gifts from Santa Claus on Christmas morning. Shopping malls bustling with Christmas shoppers and Santas in costume are a familiar sight during the holidays in Venezuelan cities.

Customs, Traditions, Ceremonies

Venezuelans, like other South American Catholics, revere the Holy Family (Mary, Joseph, and Jesus) and consider the Nativity scene, called the *Nacimiento,* the most important Christmas symbol. But they take the simple scene much further when they create the *pesebre*. This is an entire landscape, usually of their own region, with the Nacimiento placed at the center on Christmas Eve.

The family pesebre may be small enough to fit on a tabletop or large enough to fill the living room. It often includes representations of mountains, hills, rivers, waterfalls, or the sea, all made by family members from whatever material they have on hand. Venezuelans carve small figures for the scene from a lightweight wood called *aníme*.

In addition to Mary, Joseph, and the infant Jesus, the shepherds, angels, and wise men, they carve people from everyday life: workers at their jobs, farmers, even soccer players. In addition to barnyard animals, they carve other animals like dogs and cats and make modern-day machines like airplanes, cars, and motorbikes.

People begin working on their pesebres by mid-December, adding to them each day. Once finished, the pesebres remain in place until the Feast of the Candelaria on February 2. The Feast of the Candelaria, or Candlemas, refers to the biblical story of

Over-life-size figures representing the Three Wise Men are paraded through the streets of East Harlem, New York, in 1997. Venezuelans consider the Nativity scene with all its characters the most important Christmas symbol. Reproduced by permission of AP/Wide World Photos.

the purification of Mary at the temple forty days after giving birth to Jesus. It is celebrated with candle-lighting ceremonies and processions in honor of the Virgin Mary.

Candlemas is also a celebration of the day the infant Jesus was presented at the temple as "the light to lighten the Gentiles." Baby Jesus figures are removed

Hallacas (Venezuelan Meat Pies)

Ingredients

Dough

2 cups yellow cornmeal

2 cups water

1 tablespoon butter, softened

½ cup sugar

1 egg

1 tablespoon baking soda

Filling

¾ pound each of boneless, skinless chicken and pork loin, cut into small cubes

4 tablespoons vegetable oil

2 large onions, diced

4 cloves garlic, diced

1 bell pepper, diced

1½ teaspoons ground cumin

1 cup drained canned tomatoes, finely chopped

½ cup raisins, softened in warm water and drained

green olives

salt and pepper to taste

Directions

1. Make dough by boiling water and stirring in cornmeal. Reduce heat and simmer until very thick (about 15 minutes), stirring often.
2. Stir in butter, sugar, and egg. When cool, stir in baking soda.
3. Turn dough out onto a board covered with wax paper and cut dough into 16 equal pieces.
4. Heat oil and fry meat until cooked through (8 to 10 minutes), adding more oil if meat sticks to skillet.
5. Stir in onion, garlic, bell pepper, tomatoes, raisins, and cumin. Fry until tender, then add salt and pepper to taste.
6. Remove skillet from heat and divide meat mixture into 8 equal portions.
7. On a 10-inch piece of aluminum foil, press one portion of dough out to form a 5-inch circle or square, about ¼-inch thick.
8. Spoon one portion of meat mixture onto dough square and slice one or two olives onto the meat. Flatten another square of dough and place on top. Press edges together all the way around to seal.
9. Lift the sides of the foil up around the hallaca and fold foil edges together to make a pouch for steaming. Repeat for all 8 hallacas.
10. Steam hallacas in the upper basket of a large vegetable steamer for about 1 hour or until dough is fully cooked. Serve hot in the foil packets.

from the mangers of the pesebres on this day.

One form of Christmas season entertainment is visiting from house to house to look at the different pesebres. Sometimes, judges award prizes for the best ones. On Christmas Eve, or Noche Buena, the families add fresh flowers and lights to the pesebre and place the Nacimiento, or manger scene, at the center. As in some European countries, people move the Three Wise Men closer to the manger each day until Epiphany, January 6, when the figures finally reach the manger.

Foods, Recipes

A traditional Christmas dish unique to Venezuela is *hallacas* (pronounced ah-YAH-cahs), which the family serves after a midnight mass on their best china, along with the best silverware and linens. Hallacas are made from cornmeal dough and contain spices, olives, wine, and pork, chicken, or beef. They are wrapped in plantain (a kind of banana) leaves and boiled, to make a pie. Often, the whole family participates in making the hallacas. For dessert, Venezuelans like *dulce de lechoza* (pronounced DUL-say day lay-CHO-sah), a type of preserve made with green papaya and brown sugar. They also enjoy desserts made with a sweet, sticky coconut sauce.

Arts, Crafts, Games

In Venezuela and other Latin American countries, creating the pesebre is a form of art and craftsmanship. All family members, young and old, carefully choose figures to make for the season's celebration or work on the background scenery, which can be ever expanding.

The pesebre allows for each person's full artistic expression, because there are no limits on the subject matter or style of the work. Even the first carving of a young child is considered art, and each individual takes pride in his or her work because friends and neighbors stop by throughout the season to admire the family's finished creation.

Music, Dance

The music and dance form known as Gaita (pronounced GUY-tah) has become a big part of Christmas in Venezuela and is spreading to other Spanish-speaking areas. The music, long performed only in the Venezuelan state of Zulia, features thundering African drums and irreverent lyrics. It is a craze among teenagers, who attend Gaita concerts until the wee hours of the morning, as well as adults, who dance to the music at clubs.

The origins of the music are not certain, but some experts believe it comes from traditional Christmas songs called *aguinaldos* (pronounced og-gwee-NAHL-dose), introduced to Latin America centuries ago by the Spanish explorers. The term *gaita* means "bagpipes." It may have been given that name because it evokes the same kind of deep feelings in natives of Zulia as the bagpipe does among the Scottish.

Many Gaita tunes, like the classic Gaita song "The Zuliano People," are protest songs. Others are about corrupt politicians, poverty, and love. Many pay tribute to the Virgin of La Chinita, the patron saint of Zulia.

Vegetable Art in Mexico

At the Christmas market in the city of Oaxaca, Mexico, the night of December 23 has become famous as La Noche de Rabanos, or the Night of the Radishes. About thirty booths are set up along one side of the main square, and families display carved radish roots in the most fantastic shapes. Large, round, red or white radishes; long, hairy, black radishes; or smooth, white radishes are carved to look like people or animals. Different types of radishes are often combined into one carving, using toothpicks to hold them together.

Artists arrange groups of radish characters with dried flowers, other vegetables, and fruits. Some of the "human" radishes are dressed in doll clothes and jewelry. The vegetable artists create fantastic scenes, like the Nativity or other scenes from the Bible. Other *rabanos* are just strange-looking animals and people with exaggerated features. The odder the shape of the radish root, the more useful it is, for carvers use their imagination to work with the shape of the radish to create the perfect figure.

Judges choose the best carvings, and the carvers with the funniest or most creative displays get cash prizes. After the spectators have seen every display, the evening closes with fireworks around midnight. People buy the radish carvings and take them home to show off through Christmas. They are kept fresh by spraying them with water a few times each day.

Another musical tradition found in some parts of Venezuela is for people to dress as shepherds and go from house to house singing carols on La Noche Buena, Christmas Eve.

Special Role of Children, Young Adults

Children play large roles in Christmas celebrations in Latin America. They participate in plays, pageants, and processions and receive gifts on Christmas Day from Santa Claus or on Epiphany from the Three Kings, or the Three Wise Men. Sometimes children get gifts on both days, because Santa has become more and more popular through North American influence. Children also help make figures for the family's pesebre, or Nativity scene, and help prepare Christmas foods.

Roller-skating to mass

Teenagers in the Venezuelan capital of Caracas attend a special early morning mass called the Misa de Aguinaldos (Mass of the Carols), which is held daily from December 16 through December 24. Many of the streets are closed until 8 A.M. because the teens roller-skate to mass.

After the midnight mass on Christmas Eve, the main avenue is closed to traffic, and hundreds of teens roller-skate in the streets until time for morning mass. The special mass includes folk music, with a traditional band singing songs about the gifts that the wise men brought to the infant Jesus. After mass, the teens skate home to breakfast.

Just for fun, younger children often tie a string around their big toes before going to bed and let the long strings hang out the window. Every skater who passes by in the morning tugs on the strings.

Finding the *Niño*

The citizens of the historic town of Mérida, Venezuela, keep an old custom regarding the pesebre. It is called La Paradura del Niño (the Standing Up of the Christ Child), and is especially enjoyed by children.

In every home, it is the custom to stand up the figure of the Christ child in the manger scene on New Year's Day and let it remain standing until the Feast of the Candelaria on February 2. When people come to visit, they notice whether the Christ child is still standing. If a family has let their *Niño* figure fall and has not immediately returned it to a standing position, one of the guests steals the figure and takes it home to hide. To get it back, the family must give a *Paradura* party, which is a big event in the town.

The Paradura party begins in the evening with a procession through the streets. Young boys set off firecrackers to lead the way, and marchers hold candles. Children dress as Mary and Joseph, the shepherds, and the wise men, and a young girl walking before them carries a big star to represent the Star of Bethlehem.

A *conjunto* (pronounced cone-HOON-toe) band walks with the procession, but they do not play until someone finds the Christ child. Adults known as "godparents" also walk in the procession, carrying a large scarf in which they will carry the baby Jesus home when they find him. The godparents sing the Paradura carol:

> Come we now to search for the Child
> Who has been stolen from this house.
> Come now, Shepherds, come now,
> Come we altogether.

The procession stops in front of the house where the Niño is believed to be, and the family brings him out and places him in the big scarf. Then the band begins to play and sing:

> Here we find the Child
> Who we thought was lost.
> Now we'll take him to his home
> And his godparents shall carry him.

When the Christ child is finally placed back in his crib, each young child comes forward, one at a time, with a small gift for him, called an *ofrenda*. As they place the gifts at his feet, they recite a little rhyme they have learned just for the Paradura party. Each child's rhyme is about the child and his gift.

After the children have finished giving their gifts and the women have prayed, everyone goes into the house for food and drink, and the band begins to play. But before the dancing starts, the family covers the figure of the Christ child with a cloth so he will be shown no disrepect by the merrymaking.

For More Information

Morrison, Marion. *Venezuela: Enchantment of the World*. Chicago, Ill.: Children's Press, 1989.

Perl, Lila. *Piñatas and Paper Flowers: Holidays of the Americas in English and Spanish*. New York: Clarion Books, 1983.

Web sites

"Christmas in Venezuela." [Online] http://www.the-north-pole.com/around/venezuela.html (accessed on January 27, 2000).

"Worldview: Christmas in Venezuela." [Online] http://christmas.com/worldview/southamerica/venezuela.html (accessed on January 27, 2000).

Christmas Sources

Barton, David. "What's Boxing Day's Punch? Giving, Not Fighting." *The Sacramento Bee,* December 26, 1997.

Eklof, Barbara. *For Every Season: The Complete Guide to African American Celebrations Traditional to Contemporary*. New York: HarperCollins, 1997, pp. 309–11.

Esposito, Mary Ann. *Celebrations Italian Style*. New York: Hearst Books, 1995.

Field, Carol. *Celebrating Italy*. New York: William Morrow, 1990.

Green, Marian. *Traditional Celebrations, Songs, Seasonal Recipes and Things to Make*. Rockport, Mass.: Element, 1991, pp. 132–39.

Griffin, Robert H., and Ann H. Shurgin, eds. *The Folklore of World Holidays*. 2nd ed. Farmington Hills, Mich.: Gale, 1999, pp. 28, 39–40, 714–67.

Hart, Cynthia, John Grossman, and Priscilla Dunhill. *A Victorian Christmas: Joy to the World*. New York: Workman, 1990, pp. 27–29, 34–39, 44–45, 53–61.

Marcus, Harold G. *A History of Ethiopia*. Berkeley: University of California Press, 1994, p. 12.

Marcus, Rebecca B., and Judith Marcus. *Fiesta Time in Mexico*. Champaign, Ill.: Garrard Publishing, 1990. pp. 31–52.

Nash, Edgar S. "Why We Do What We Do at Christmas." *The Saturday Evening Post,* November-December 1993, pp. 35–36, 70–73.

Naythons, Matthew. *Christmas Around the World*. San Francisco: Collins Publishers, 1996, pp. 26–35, 186.

Pankhurst, Richard. *The Ethiopians*. Malden, Mass.: Blackwell Publishing, 1998, pp. 48–49, 52–53, 91.

Restad, Penne L. *Christmas in America: A History*. New York: Oxford University Press, 1995, pp. 3–28, 45–74, 109–22, 146–150.

Romantschuk, Thomas. "Helsinki: Welcome to Santa Land Inc." *Europe,* December 1998/January 1999, pp. 43–44.

Santino, Jack. *All Around the Year: Holidays and Celebrations in American Life*. Urbana and Chicago: University of Illinois Press, 1994, pp. 49–50, 178–205.

Streep, Peg, Jane Lahr, and Leslie Garisto, eds. *An American Christmas: A Celebration of Our Heritage from Around the World*. In Philosophical Library. New York: Allied Books, 1989, pp. 10–19, 116–18, 152–59, 163–66.

Thompson, Sue Ellen. *Holiday Symbols 1998*. Detroit, Mich.: Omnigraphics, 1998, pp. 69–74.

Webb, Lois Sinaiko. *Holidays of the World Cookbook for Students*. Phoenix, Ariz.: Oryx Press, 1995, pp. 7–8, 95, 126, 183–84, 237.

Web sites

"Aspects of the Antebellum Christmas." [Online] http://www.connerprairie.org/xmas.html (accessed on February 24, 2000).

"Christmas in Norway." [Online] http://www.julenissen.no/jul-norge.html (accessed on February 24, 2000).

"The History of Christmas." [Online] http://www.worldbook.com/fun/holidays/html/history.htm (accessed on February 24, 2000).

"The History of Christmas Seals." [Online] http://www.christmasseals.org/history.html (accessed on February 24, 2000).

"Italy: Buon Natale." [Online] http://www.californiamall.com/holidaytraditions/traditions-italy.htm (accessed on February 24, 2000).

"Origins of Christmas Customs & Traditions Around the World." [Online] http://www.bconnex.net/~mbuchana/realms/christmas/origindx.html (accessed on February 24, 2000).

Index

Italic type indicates volume numbers;
boldface type indicates entries and their page numbers;
(ill.) indicates illustrations;
(box) indicates information found in sidebar boxes.